"Barbara Newman's *Helping Kids Include Kids with Disabilities* is thoughtful, accessible, and eminently helpful in offering practical tools for Sunday school teachers and youth ministers to create an inclusive environment within their churches. Although this book is short, which makes it all the more readable, Newman somehow manages to pack it full of information about mental and physical disabilities in the context of Christian theology. Every church library should have a copy, and every director of youth and children's ministries should refer to it often."

—Amy Julia Becker, author of *A Good and Perfect Gift: Faith, Expectations, and a Little Girl Named Penny* (Bethany Books, 2011; named one of Publisher's Weekly's Top Books of 2011) and *Why I Am Both Spiritual and Religious.*

"Barbara's book reminds us that relationships lie at the heart of an inclusive community. Her straightforward guide offers practical ideas for connecting kids with and without disabilities in ways that are likely to foster friendships and faith."

—Erik Carter, Ph.D., associate professor of special education, Vanderbilt University

"Another Barbara Newman 'home run!' As always, Barb's biblically solid material is practical, positive, and powerful. This is a 'must-have' resource for anyone involved in children's ministry."

—Stephanie O. Hubach, Mission to North America special needs ministries director, Presbyterian Church in America; author of *Same Lake, Different Boat: Coming Alongside People Touched by Disability.*

BARBARA J. NEWMAN

helping kids include kids with disabilities

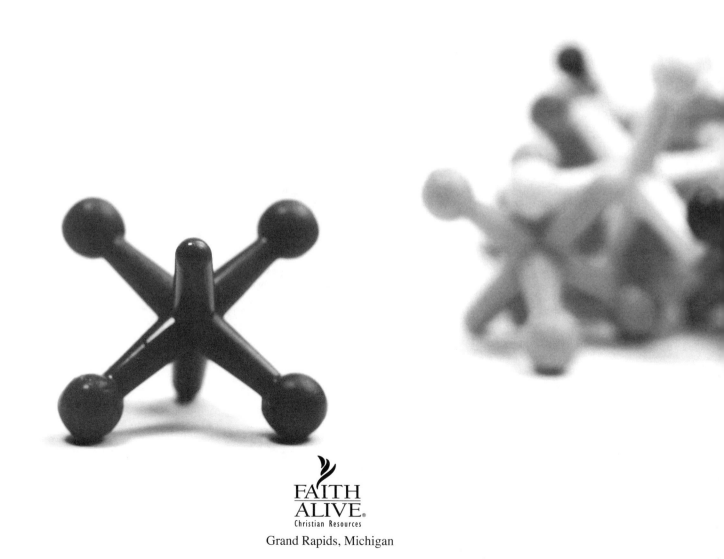

FAITH
ALIVE®
Christian Resources

Grand Rapids, Michigan

Cover design: Pete Euwema

Printed in the United States of America.

We welcome your comments. Call us at 1-800-333-8300 or email us at editors@faithaliveresources.org.

Library of Congress Cataloging-in-Publication Data
Newman, Barbara J.
  Helping kids include kids with disabilities / Barbara J. Newman.
        p. cm.
    Includes bibliographical references.
    ISBN 978-1-56212-777-0
    1. Church work with children.
    2. Developmentally disabled children Religious life. I. Title BV4461.3.N48 2001 259'.44—dc21
                                                                        2001023690

10 9 8 7 6 5 4 3 2 1

Dedicated with love to my dear family:
- my husband Barry Newman,
- and our sons John and James Newman.

Contents

Foreword

How is your son enjoying Sunday school?" I asked the parents at the end of our parent-teacher conference. A heavy sigh prefaced their answer. When their son with autism was three, the parents explained, he attended children's worship for the first time. After class, a weary worker returned their son and said, "Please don't bring him back to this class. We can't handle him." For the next four years, one parent attended church and one parent stayed home with their son. Too old to qualify for the nursery but unable to sit through a service, their young son, they felt, had no place in their congregation.

A young adolescent with a mild intellectual disability could hardly wait to start his first year of boys' club at church. Although he was unable to read, he saw each of his older brothers making Pinewood Derby cars, and he longed for the day when he would be able to participate. The great day finally arrived. But after the first night of boys' club, the leader called the boy's parents and asked them not to send him again. He was unable to read the materials, and the leaders didn't know how to handle that.

A congregation had been praying for several months. A little girl was having uncontrollable seizures, and the doctors had run out of medications to prescribe. The girl's church family cried out to God, asking that these frequent attacks in her brain would stop. And God answered those prayers. The seizures stopped, but the girl faced years of therapy and special education to help her grow and learn. Unaware of the extent of her brain injury, and not sharing in the painstaking routines of daily therapy, the church family happily celebrated God's answer to prayer.

At the same time, the girl's parents grew resentful and angry that God would allow their daughter to face such challenges. Now, more than ever, they needed support and care from their church family.

Fortunately, each of these three stories had a happy ending. In each case, the child's parents and their school contacted the church. Each pastor they contacted was truly sorry the incidents in question had happened, and each was eager to better understand the child's gifts and needs. The boy with autism was assigned a special helper so that his parents could worship together. The child in boys' club had a rotating buddy each week who read and wrote with him before they both enjoyed the craft. With the parents' permission, the pastor of the little girl with seizures updated the congregation so they would better understand her needs and her family could continue to receive appropriate support.

I believe that church—a place where children with disabilities and their families desperately need to experience belonging and inclusion—can sometimes be a place of misunderstanding and perceived rejection. But that can change. After twenty-seven years of working with CLC Network (Christian Learning Center) and serving as the church services division director, as well as a special education coordinator for an inclusive education program at Zeeland Christian School in Michigan, I'm convinced that God can use what we have learned in the classroom setting and in church settings to help congregations better enfold children and adults with disabilities.

This book explains some of the methods we use to help carve out a place of belonging for students with disabilities at Zeeland Christian School, as well as in a variety of church settings. As part of CLC Network, we welcome children of parents who want a Christian education for their family. Whatever their children's unique gifts and needs are, we attempt to provide programs and people to meet them in our school. It's my hope and prayer that the ideas in this book will also better equip churches to welcome children with disabilities and give them a place of respect and honor in their congregation.

A Word about Labels

Children with disabilities usually have been given some type of label that describes a medical condition or an educational need. This label can help teachers and other caregivers better understand that child's gifts and meet that child's needs. As you read about various kinds of descriptors and designations in this book, please remember these five things about labels:

- **See the person, not the label.** A child may have a great sense of humor and be a good runner and have an intellectual disability. It's easy to look at an individual with a disability and see "Down syndrome Ryan" or "spina bifida Blake," but that is certainly not in line with what God teaches in his Word. That person is "Ryan, who is made in God's image to fill a specific purpose in God's kingdom, who has been given gifts to offer others in the body of Christ, who also happens to have Down syndrome." We should always see a disability in the context of God's amazing design for that person and in the context of Christ's body, the church. Kathie Snow has done some excellent work in this area. You can find her brief but very helpful article on people-first language at disabilityisnatural.com/images/PDF/pfl-sh09.pdf.

- **Never attempt to attach a label yourself.** You may read about autism spectrum disorder, for example, and notice that a child in your group has many of those characteristics. For you to apply the material in this book in your Sunday school class without a proper diagnosis and permission from the child's parents could potentially be very hurtful to that child and to his or her family.

- **Labels change.** This book uses labels and terms that are considered preferred usage at the time of printing. But those labels and terms change often. Please also be aware that states differ in the labels and terms they use for educational purposes to describe children who have disabilities, and these terms can change over time too. For example, a child who is called "cognitively impaired" by a school system in one state or province might be called "developmentally delayed" in another. Keep this in mind as you adapt this material for use in your own state or province.

- **Start with the child.** When planning for a child with a disability in a church setting, never begin by understanding the child's medical or educational label. Always begin by getting to know that child. The plans and ideas you develop need to wrap around that child's unique gift areas and need areas. While it's helpful to know some general information about areas of disability, the most important way to begin is by getting to know Maria or Blake or Tamika.

- **There's more to learn.** Keep in mind that this book offers only an overview of various kinds of disabilities. There is much more material available about each highlighted area. If you want to learn more, start by checking into some of the resources listed at the back of this book.

Dedication and Acknowledgments

I dedicate this book to my family. I want to give special thanks to my husband, Barry, who sharpens me in my walk with God and who has spent many years being my partner in ministry. I thank God for you and the ways you continue to influence my life. Thanks also to my children, John and James, who continue to teach me about each person being a unique creation of God and who also delight in accepting, welcoming, understanding, and befriending persons with disabilities. I see God's heart in both of you.

I would also like to thank the following people for their encouragement and for helping me to better understand this information and put it into a book:

All of the students at Zeeland Christian School, who have allowed me to learn with and from them.

Doug Bouman, psychologist for CLC Network in Grand Rapids, Michigan, who taught me to think in greens and pinks.

Leslie Drahos, Carol Gray, and the consultants from Ottawa Area Intermediate School District, who have taught me so much about children with autism spectrum disorder.

Dr. Thomas B. Hoeksema, William VanDyk, Richard "Bear" Berends, and Jan DeJonge, who have been so influential in my life as a special educator.

Dr. Andrew Bandstra, professor emeritus of New Testament and Theology at Calvin Theological Seminary, who also happens to be my father and who has helped and supported me in these endeavors.

My dear mother, Mae Ruth Bandstra, who passed away five years ago. Her actions and words about kindness, acceptance, and love continue to influence my actions and words on a daily basis.

My colleagues at Zeeland Christian School, from whom I learn daily.

May God use this material to build up and strengthen the church. To God be the glory.

CHAPTER 1

Information: The Key to Understanding Children with Disabilities

Each day in my classroom, there are times when a colleague speaks to me and I do not respond. A person makes a comment, and I do not even turn around and listen. When that happens, the person might interpret my failure to respond as rudeness. "Why won't she answer my question? How rude." On the other hand, she might think that I'm signifying disapproval. "I wonder if she doesn't agree with what I said. Is that why she's ignoring me?"

So you can imagine what a difference it made to my colleagues (and me!) when I shared an important piece of information: as a result of a complication with my pregnancy, I experienced the early onset of hearing loss. Although one of my ears functions within the typical range, the other ear has moderate hearing loss. For that reason, I do not always hear the words or sounds that others hear. People need to get my attention visually if I do not respond. I would much rather give out this information to the people in my life than deal with the consequences of being misinterpreted or misunderstood.

Sharing that piece of information allowed my friends and colleagues to correctly assess my actions. It's as though the information gave them a special pair of glasses that enabled them to interpret my actions correctly.

Wearing the Right Glasses Helps Us See Better

Jesus was a master at planting information at critical times. For example, one day the teachers of the law had in their custody a woman caught in adultery. They were about to stone her to death as required by the law of Moses. But the woman was spared because Jesus gave a different pair of glasses to those who were holding the stones: "Let any one of you who is without sin be the first to throw a stone at her" (John 8:7). Jesus' words allowed the people to take a new look at the situation.

We can all benefit from wearing glasses that allow us to see better. Here's an example. Perhaps you've sat in church behind a family with a particularly squirmy child. Maybe you've found yourself thinking, "Why can't those people control that kid? A bit of discipline would go a long way. Parents are way too permissive these days." If you'd been wearing the glasses that let you recognize that this "undisciplined" child has a condition called attention deficit/hyperactivity disorder (AD/HD), you wouldn't make the same judgment. Understanding the neurological basis of a child's actions allows us to see more clearly and respond with compassion, not judgment.

I have found that accurate information is one of the most powerful tools in creating a successful program for including children with disabilities in school and church. I believe that leaders, children, and parents of peers need to be given the right glasses in order to practice greater acceptance and understanding.

Understanding God's Design

The most critical information people must have relates to understanding God's heart for children and God's design for the body of believers. God has uniquely crafted each person, and each has an important place in the body of Christ. We are called to accept each person as a full member of the body. As we recognize God's heart for the kind of community where "The eye cannot say to the hand, 'I don't need you!' And the head cannot say to the feet, 'I don't need you!' On the contrary, those parts of the body that seem to be weaker are indispensable" (1 Cor. 12:21-22), we gain a vision for including persons with disabilities that far exceeds any educational practice or legal ruling. Christians embrace the principle of acceptance embodied in inclusive community as a part of doing God's will. This information about God's will needs to be woven into all of our preparation and communication.

Tony and Rick

But we need to know more than God's design for the body of believers. We need to understand more about how God designed us and the other people in our lives. A study we did at school using sociograms (diagrams that show the structure of interpersonal relationships in groups) helped us understand the impact information can have on kids' acceptance of their peers with disabilities.

Here's how it worked. Tony, a first-grader, was diagnosed with autism. He was supported with an individualized curriculum, an alternate environment when needed, and a circle of friends. To encourage

Boys

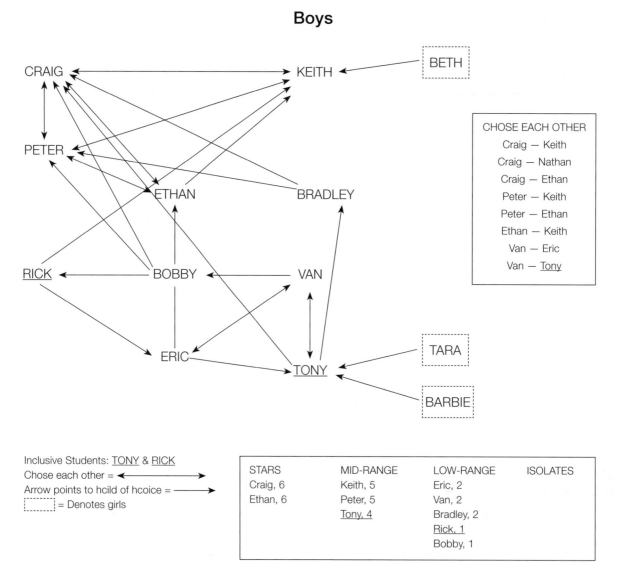

CHOSE EACH OTHER
Craig — Keith
Craig — Nathan
Craig — Ethan
Peter — Keith
Peter — Ethan
Ethan — Keith
Van — Eric
Van — Tony

Inclusive Students: TONY & RICK
Chose each other = ◄——————►
Arrow points to hcild of hcoice = ——————►
⌐¦¦¦¦¦¦¦¬ = Denotes girls

STARS	MID-RANGE	LOW-RANGE	ISOLATES
Craig, 6	Keith, 5	Eric, 2	
Ethan, 6	Peter, 5	Van, 2	
	Tony, 4	Bradley, 2	
		Rick, 1	
		Bobby, 1	

—Used by permission of Karen Zoetewey, Zeeland Christian School

the children in Tony's class to form friendships with him, I talked about Tony's gifts and explained autism to the children. I told them what to expect from Tony. We held ongoing "circle" meetings to discuss what was going well and to identify problem areas. All of this information helped to equip Tony's classmates with a pair of glasses for understanding his behavior. The lenses were changed throughout the year as needed.

As you can see in the sociogram on page 12, Tony was in the mid-range list of children chosen by others when asked "Who do you want to work with?" Despite his occasionally aggressive actions, delayed speaking skills, and differences in social skills, the other kids chose him several times.

During the course of the school year, Rick, another child from that same class, was diagnosed with a very rare disorder called Landau-Kleffner syndrome. Because the diagnostic process took so long, Rick was not given an official place in the special education program. As a result, his classmates did not have the same opportunity to understand his actions. As you can see from the diagram, Rick was chosen by only one person, putting him in the low-range category.

Between first and second grade, Rick was placed in a special education support group that included individualized curriculum, an alternate environment when needed, and a circle of friends. A second sociogram from the next year showed that Rick's acceptance level soared in the second grade. That year he was chosen many times by others, despite continued behavioral concerns from grade 1. Rick was now a "star." Although other factors may have been involved, it seems clear that Rick benefited from his peers' knowledge of his gifts and needs and from what they had learned about Landau-Kleffner syndrome. That information allowed them to understand Rick and be his friends.

Families Need Glasses Too

At Zeeland Christian School, not only do we give information to the classmates of kids with disabilities, we also send information home to all families in the class (after we receive written permission from the parents of the child). This information gives the families of all the kids in the class the glasses they need to support classroom friendship and understand the special situations that can develop.

Knowing that those families had the right kind of glasses helped us deal with an incident involving Tony, the first-grader with autism we mentioned earlier. Biting was sometimes a problem with Tony. In explaining autism to the kids in Tony's class, I said that each one of us has a set of keys designed by God to unlock certain sections of our brain. We have a key for moving and talking and making friends. Many of our keys look alike, but some of our keys are different. Tony already had his reading key, but some of the other children did not. For Tony, however, his understanding of how to play on the playground was a key he did not yet have. I wondered with them if Tony might get his playground key this year and if they might get a reading key.

The next day at recess, Tony bit his friend Ryan. Ryan calmly walked to find his teacher, with his aggressor in tow. Without tears, Ryan explained to his teacher that they needed to find Tony's key for not biting.

Because the bite had broken Ryan's skin, our principal asked me to phone his parents. Based on the letter I had sent home about Tony, autism, and God's desire for us to live in community with those who have autism, his parents were very understanding about the incident. A potentially very difficult situation was avoided based on the "glasses" that we had given the whole school community at the beginning of the year.

The same need for information applies to teachers, church group leaders, and volunteers. We expect them to have the skills to intervene with integrity in a variety of situations. Each one of these frontline workers needs to be equipped with accurate information about the child's individual strengths and needs, as well as information about his or her area of disability.

Helping Kids Understand Themselves

Often the most overlooked of all those who participate in caring for children with disabilities are the children themselves. In addition to giving information to parents, teachers, and peers, we need to make sure that we give children with disabilities the information they need to understand why they think and act the way they do. This enables them to advocate for themselves and allows them to know their own boundaries, challenges, and strengths.

In the next chapter, "The Mind That's Mine," you'll find strategies to accurately and positively help kids understand how God creates each one of us with unique strengths and challenges. God "knit me together in my mother's womb" (Ps. 139:13) and I am "fearfully and wonderfully made" (Ps. 139:14). I believe we honor our Creator as we marvel at the new pattern God created for each precious person.

How Can This Book Help?

This book is designed to help your church or school become a welcoming place for people with disabilities. To help you find the information you need, I have prepared materials on six specific areas of disability that are common in church settings. For each of these areas you'll find a basic fact sheet for the leader or volunteer, a lesson plan you can adapt for preschool through grade 6, and a sample letter to families you can send home with the child's classmates.

You'll also find two separate sections that deal specifically with school-age diagnoses as well as severe and multiple disabilities. Be aware that dual diagnosis is often a reality: a child with Down syndrome may also have autism; a child with autism may also have a seizure disorder.

For help with tailoring any lesson plan to the abilities of the children in your class, see the Activity Substitution Guide on page 73.

The book also includes a lesson plan suitable for promoting acceptance with middle school and high school students. All of this information is preceded by the chapter called "The Mind That's Mine,"

which will help you explain to each child a bit more about the way his or her own brain works. Be sure to read chapter 3, "Guidelines for Churches," before going on to read the section on the specific type of disability you are dealing with.

It's my hope that the information in this book will allow many children to experience a greater sense of belonging at church. I will have succeeded if these pages equip you with glasses that help you see a child with a disability less as a spectacle than as an integral part of your group setting and of the body of Christ.

An Important Note about Sharing Information

Sharing information on disabilities in general and about particular people with disabilities is vital to helping others understand and support them. But I can't stress enough that you must always obtain permission from the person and his or her parents or guardians before you do so. Your primary concern must be to protect that person's dignity, and if there is some information that the family is not comfortable sharing, you must maintain absolute confidentiality.

CHAPTER 2

The Mind That's Mine*
Helping Kids Understand How Our Minds Work

Sitting across the table from me was a seventh-grade boy. Nathan's mother had asked me to spend some time with him to figure out why he was failing all his classes. "He seems so bright," she kept saying. So, armed with my testing materials, previous school reports, and some bottled water and snacks, I spent a morning with Nathan and his mother.

After I administered some tests, I explained to Nathan a little about how his mind works. I began by explaining my own mind's strengths and weaknesses and then moved on to his. I was able to point out that his areas of visual thinking and memory were outstanding, along with his ability to draw. The areas of paying attention and language were difficult for him. I explained how Concerta—a medication he had previously refused—works, and also detailed how his particular difficulty in language might play out in class. Armed with this information, Nathan started taking his medication. He advocated for himself with his teachers and pulled his grades up to a "B" average.

Clearly, there is power in information. Many children, given an accurate description of their own wondrous thought processes, can begin to make better choices for themselves. How would you feel if you were examined by a medical doctor who then proceeded to share the results of the exam with everyone but you? You'd be upset, right? In fact, it's illegal for doctors to do that, but something similar frequently happens when children are assessed at school.

Doug Bouman, a psychologist for CLC Network, has devised an excellent tool for sharing such information with parents and children (adapted from Dr. Mel Levine in his book *Educational Care*, *2nd Edition*, Educators Publishing Service, 2001).

Shown on the next page is a chain link diagram that represents different neurological processes detailed by Levine in his book. Bouman uses this representation not necessarily to share test scores but to paint an accurate neurological picture of strengths and weaknesses. Using this information, a teacher can plan a program that enhances a child's strengths and targets weaknesses.

Although some schools are developing programs and activities to help older elementary children understand their neurological profile, I believe younger children can also understand the fact that they are made in a special way: some things come easily to them and some things are more difficult.

This knowledge, I believe, is especially important in inclusive communities at school or church. Children will flourish in an atmosphere that affirms that they are each a unique imagebearer of God. In that context, children can best understand that they are "God's handiwork, created in Christ Jesus to do good works" (Eph. 2:10). Think of the children in your group as a field of brilliant wildflowers—each one beautifully different from the next.

---

*This phrase is used by Mel Levine in his book *Educational Care*.

Multifact Assessment Planning System (M.A.P.S.)
Neurodevelopmental "Links" ("The Mind That's Mine")

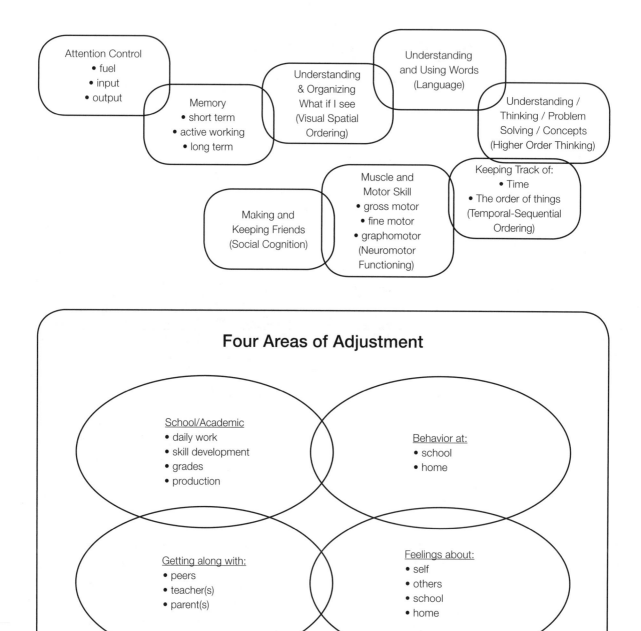

Attention Control
- fuel
- input
- output

Memory
- short term
- active working
- long term

Understanding & Organizing What if I see (Visual Spatial Ordering)

Understanding and Using Words (Language)

Understanding / Thinking / Problem Solving / Concepts (Higher Order Thinking)

Keeping Track of:
- Time
- The order of things (Temporal-Sequential Ordering)

Muscle and Motor Skill
- gross motor
- fine motor
- graphomotor (Neuromotor Functioning)

Making and Keeping Friends (Social Cognition)

Four Areas of Adjustment

School/Academic
- daily work
- skill development
- grades
- production

Behavior at:
- school
- home

Getting along with:
- peers
- teacher(s)
- parent(s)

Feelings about:
- self
- others
- school
- home

—Reprinted by permission of Doug Bouman, CLC Network, Grand Rapids, Michigan.

LESSON PLAN
The Mind That's Mine

Notes

This lesson plan, adapted from Doug Bouman's chain link model, can be used in a church group or classroom setting with elementary-age children. Please remember that this does not take the place of a professional assessment. It is a way to allow each child to begin to see the wonderful design God used in creating him or her as a unique person.

You'll want to tailor this lesson plan to the ages of your children—check the sidebars for suggestions for adapting the lesson plan for younger and older children. You should also tailor this lesson plan to the abilities of the children in your group, so every child can participate in a meaningful way. Need some help? See the Activity Substitution Guide on page 73.

Plan on taking about twenty minutes for this lesson plan. Consider blending it with a lesson on creation, on being made in the image of God, or on there being many gifts but one body. It's a great way to build community and understanding.

Materials

- black ink pad
- photocopy paper, one sheet per student
- baby wipes
- several magnifying glasses
- rope or clothesline, enough to make two large circles on the floor
- banana
- apple
- picture book with no words
- skills pictures (Patterns, pp.76-77), photocopy one set per child and one set for yourself

- brain picture (Patterns, p. 78), photocopy one per child

Step 1

■ On photocopy paper, have each child make a set of fingerprints using the black ink pad. Clean inky fingers with baby wipes.

■ Invite the children to use magnifying glasses to compare their fingerprints with those of others in the class. Can they find another student whose fingerprints match their own?

■ Talk about why police officers take fingerprints. Say that if police officers could get brainprints, that would be even better. Like our fingerprints, our brains are also very different and special. No one has a brain just like your brain. We won't be able to take a photo of our brains today, but we can find out a little bit about what our brains are like.

Step 2

■ Make two large rope circles on the floor. Tell the children that you would like to find out more about their brains by seeing what they like to do. Put a banana by one circle and an apple by the other circle. Invite the children to stand in the circle that shows which fruit they like the most (or point to that circle if they have mobility issues).

■ Let the children make another choice. Show them the picture book without saying a word. Let them see each picture. Then put the book away and tell them the story with no pictures. Explain that some of us have a brain that likes to

17

learn by seeing and others of us like to learn by listening. Ask them to go to or point to one circle if they like to learn by seeing, and the other circle if they like to learn by hearing.

- Verbally present other choices and allow the children to go to or point to the circle that represents their favorite. (For example, play with Legos or listen to a story, play with friends or play alone).

- Hold up your copy of the skills pictures to introduce the topic of what our brains are responsible for doing. Our brains help us do things like pay attention to our teachers, talk, remember, use our eyes, use our ears, understand time, solve problems, write, move our arms and legs, know and love Jesus, and make friends.

- Tell the children something about your own brain. What things do you like to do best? What things are you good at? What things are hard for you to do? Be honest with them about your strengths and weaknesses, likes and dislikes.

Step 3

- Distribute the brain picture and a copy of the skills pictures to each child. Ask the children to cut apart the skills pictures and glue two or three that represent their own strengths on the top part of the brain picture page. Then they can glue two or three that represent their weaknesses on the bottom of the brain picture page. Do this exercise yourself as the children are working.

- Give each child a chance to choose one of their strengths and tell the group how they could use that strength to help God and others. If they seem hesitant, get them started by telling about the strengths God gave you that help you do the things you're good at. Help the children if they get stuck, and affirm each answer and each child as a gift from God: "Yes, I see you making lots of friends and helping others." "Yes, you could use your drawing skills to create things for others to enjoy."

- Read and discuss Ephesians 2:10: "For we are God's handiwork, created in Christ Jesus to do good works, which God prepared in advance for us to do." Ask what good works the children think God may have prepared for them to do. End with a prayer of thanksgiving for the way God created each boy and girl in your class.

Adaptations for Younger Children

Younger children may need a bit more guidance from you in identifying their own strengths and weaknesses. As they are working with the pictures and choosing things that are easy and things that are more difficult, walk around the room and mention strengths that you have seen in each child.

At the conclusion of the lesson, it may be helpful to state what you see as each child's strength and how he or she could use that gift in service to God.

Adaptations for Older Children

Instead of distributing the skills pictures to cut apart, you may wish to have the children draw or write directly on the brain picture to represent their strengths and weaknesses.

As part of step 3, explain that we can see other people's strengths too, and it's important to tell them about the great strengths that God has given them. Have each child write his or her name on the top of a paper. Ask the children to pass their paper to the person on their right, and have that person write down something special about the person whose name is on the paper. (Some ideas: "You are a good friend." "You draw well." "You can talk about Jesus." "You memorize words well," and so on.) Continue passing the papers until the children have had a chance to write on each one and their own paper comes back to them. Let them read and enjoy what others have written about them.

CHAPTER 3

Guidelines for Churches

n the chapters that follow, you will find specific information about a variety of disabilities. Before you launch into that information, I suggest you take some time to think about how your church welcomes people with disabilities. Ask yourself these questions:

Do the members of our church have the information they need in order to understand and enfold people with disabilities?

Are our facilities and programs accessible to people with various disabilities?

Are we willing to make changes to allow people with disabilities to participate fully in worship, education, and fellowship?

Do our church's communications (bulletin, website, and so on) make it clear that people with disabilities are welcome?

Do we mirror Jesus' open arms as he says, "Let the children come to me, and do not hinder them, for the kingdom of heaven belongs to such as these" (Matt. 19:14)?

When a family that includes a child with a disability begins attending your church, don't assume they know their child is welcome—tell them! Invite the child to attend the children's ministry programs, and communicate what supports and accommodations are available. Find out what the child's gifts are and find ways to use those gifts. Find out what the child's needs are, and plan ways to meet them. Evaluate the accessibility of your facilities and programs. Help the other children in the group better understand that friend and the area of disability so

they can welcome, learn from, and support that individual in appropriate ways.

This chapter includes general guidelines for presenting information to children, a parent interview guide you can use to find out the gifts and needs of a child, and an individual planning form you can fill out for each child with a disability so that you can begin to make the necessary modifications to your church education program.

In order to make sure that the techniques described in this book transfer from a Christian school setting to a church setting, I have worked closely with many churches. Most of the guidelines and forms come from these church/school partnerships. The results have been gratifying as parents, teachers, and church education leaders have worked together to develop meaningful strategies for including children with disabilities in their congregations.

One key component of successfully integrating children with disabilities in a church setting is appointing one person to be the coordinator for children with unique gifts and needs. This person can be part of a planning team, together with the Sunday school teacher (or girls' club mentor, or whatever the situation may be) and a parent. As needs arise, the coordinator can help obtain the necessary resources. Although the coordinator never replaces the vital contact between the teacher and parent, he or she can help pass on crucial information from leader to leader so that the parents experience continuity in the care of their child. Each year can build on the previous year, as opposed to starting from scratch.

The coordinator should

- become aware of each child who will need special support within the church education program and extend a personal welcome to each child and his or her family.

- work with the child's parents to identify that child's strengths and challenges, along with his or her educational designation or medical diagnosis.

- communicate what supports and accommodations are available for the child.

- with the permission of parents or guardians, photocopy the appropriate information sections of this book that apply to each child and distribute them to leaders, volunteers, or others involved in the child's church life.

- set up a time to meet with parents and leaders to fill out the parent interview sheet, as well as the individualized plan for the year to come. If a child is in Sunday school as well as another church group, all the people involved should meet together. Make plans to meet together again to discuss the child's individual program, progress, and acceptance.

- contact the child's schoolteacher or special education teacher for more information, with parental permission.

- work with other church leaders to ensure a welcoming environment for people with disabilities.

For a more comprehensive set of guidelines for a church coordinator, along with specialized forms for developing an individualized plan, *The G.L.U.E. Training Manual* is an excellent resource (Kimberly S. Luurtsema and Barbara J. Newman, CLC Network, 2009—visit clcnetwork.org to order this downloadable resource).

As part of your planning with parents, volunteers, or other program leaders, you'll want to decide whether the child's class or group would benefit from the lesson plans in this book that follow each specific area of disability. If so, decide whether the coordinator, leader, or a parent should guide this lesson. Read over the letter to families at the end of each section, and consider adapting it to send home to the families of the child's peers.

Plan on taking about twenty minutes for the lesson plan that follows each specific disability area. You may want to incorporate the lesson into an existing lesson. I recommend using the lesson plans at the beginning of the year. You may want to modify the lesson from year to year, but do call attention to the child's need for friendship and understanding each year.

As you become more familiar with these materials, you will find that you can mix and match lesson plans, to a certain extent, to explain an area of uniqueness. For example, the idea of using a set of car keys embedded in the lesson plan on autism spectrum disorder might be adapted to fit when teaching children about a child with an intellectual disability.

The most important starting point is to get to know the child and then fit the ideas in the lesson plan to allow others to delight in Juan or Marta or Jane. It's less important to teach children about a disability area than to teach children about the wondrous gift Juan is to our church. As the children learn more about Juan, notice how each of their lives is transformed in the process.

General Guidelines for Presenting Information to Peers

- Present information about a child with a disability with the child present whenever possible. This teaches children that the disability and accompanying differences are things they can discuss openly. The material that follows is designed to be used in this way. Be aware that there may be cases, however, where it would be detrimental to include the child, especially in the case of children with school-based disabilities or behavior challenges and disorders. Use your judgment on this.

- Be positive and honest.

- Seek input from a parent or guardian (see sample Parent Interview Guide, p. 22) before choosing what to share with the class.

- You *must* get written permission from the child's parents before talking to peers or sending a letter home to the families of the child's peers (see "Letter to Family" in the section on each disability area). Be sure to communicate to your class that the information is being presented with the consent of the child and his or her parents or caregivers. Also, do personalize the lesson and the letter to reflect the unique gifts and needs of the child.

- Keep communicating. One burst of information is not enough. You will need to talk openly throughout the year. Teach children to be positive and honest in their comments. "Wow, it's great that Joe is learning to interact, but it hurts when he hits. Who has some ideas of what we can do to help Joe?" or "I agree it's hard to know what to do when Maria uses such a loud voice. I know her ears are very sensitive to noises and when she is afraid something might hurt her ears, she starts to cry and call out. I wonder how we might help Maria with some of the sounds and help her feel safer in our room?"

- Set aside special times to talk about God's attitude toward those with disabilities. Study the Bible. Some children have incredible, miraculous stories of their own. Share these. Invite a parent to come in to talk about the child and the miracle.

- Use good children's literature to launch discussion. Preview the material to make sure it is positive and honest.

- Send notes home occasionally to encourage the child and his or her parents. Children of all ages love getting personal notes from people they look up to. A simple note that says, "Sara is an exceptional friend to Lee. She is kind but also expects a lot from him. I am so thankful for her presence in this group" will encourage parents too.

- Be specific in your feedback with children. Tell them what you like about an interaction or time segment. "You zipped up Sean's coat, but you reminded him to put on his own boots. I like the way you remembered what we can do for Sean and what he can do for himself."

- Encourage friendship. Once you have given children the information about a child with a disability, encourage them to be part of that child's "circle of friends." While this is a popular concept in many school settings that include children with disabilities, instituting a circle of friends in a church setting might encourage children to surround that friend and provide opportunities for companionship and understanding, both inside church and outside. For more information on circles of friends, consider the resource book *Circle of Friends Manual* (Barbara J. Newman, CLC Network, 2010—visit clcnetwork.org to order). This manual will give you additional ideas beyond the initial lesson plans found here. These ideas will encourage lasting friendships as children discover the mutual blessing of being in relationship with one another.

Parent Interview Guide

Use this guide to get accurate information from the parent or guardian of a child with a disability. Here is a list of suggested questions; you may want to substitute or add some of your own.

1. I want to make your child's experience in this church group the best possible. What activities and people does your child enjoy?

2. What are your child's gifts and strengths?

3. What areas are difficult for your child?

4. Please tell me a bit about your child's story and his or her area of disability.

5. Can you think of any physical modifications that I could make in our meeting area? (You may want to visit the meeting area with the parent or guardian.)

6. Does your child have any physical differences that would be helpful for me to understand?

7. Does your child take any medications I should know about?

8. Does your child have any food allergies or other allergies?

9. Will your child need help in taking care of him- or herself? For example, will your child need help with the bathroom?

10. How does your child learn best (through words, pictures, role-playing)?

11. In what ways does your child communicate best (writing, pointing, signs or gestures, words)?

12. What behavior management strategies have you found most helpful with your child?

13. What do you hope this environment will do for your child?

14. Is there anything you would like me to tell the other children specifically?

15. Is there anything else you would like me to know?

(You may wish to ask a bit more about the child's disability, age of onset, or cause of the disability based on the specific gifts and needs of the child.)

Individual Planning Form

Individual Plan for _____

Date _____ Child's leaders(s) _____

Parent(s) _____

Church coordinator _____

Child's areas of strength:

Child's areas of difficulty:

Physical accommodations (special seating, lighting, accessibility issues, break area, emergency call systems, and so on):

Staffing accommodations (co-teacher, assistant, nurse, one-to-one tutor, assigned buddy for each meeting, and so on):

Curriculum accommodations (material presented at a different level, review by parents, pencil with grip, limited written work, no oral reading, shorter memory work, and so on):

Important reminders (medications, emergency procedures, allergies, and so on):

CHAPTER 4
Specific Areas of Disability

Autism Spectrum Disorder

Behavioral Challenges and Disorders

Hearing Impairment

Intellectual Disability

Physical Disability

Visual Impairment

Autism Spectrum Disorder

Note: This unit on autism spectrum disorder includes the following:

■ Basic Fact Sheet

■ Lesson Plan

■ Letter to Families

Please note that each child is an individual. The categories we use to describe children are helpful only in explaining general characteristics. Children with autism spectrum disorder vary greatly in their gifts, as well as in the significance of the impact of their areas of difference. Please be sure to contact the child's parent or guardian to obtain more specific information about the child in your group.

Autism Spectrum Disorder

n the 1980s, autism spectrum disorder (ASD) was diagnosed in about 1 in 10,000 children. That figure is closer to 1 in 100 today. Most of us know an individual with ASD or have watched a TV show or interview featuring a story about autism. Even though many of us have a clear mental picture of an individual with ASD, it's important to remember that when you've met one child with autism, you've met exactly that—*one* child with autism. As is true of any area of disability, the range of ability and severity in ASD is very great. Within that diversity, however, we can identify some common threads.

Generally, children with ASD have differences in six areas:

Social interaction and social understanding. So many of us can walk into a group of people and nearly instantly know how to act and what to say. Children with ASD, however, find that difficult. Either avoiding social situations or making many social errors or blunders, children with ASD may benefit from being taught very specifically how to act in a given situation, including in church settings.

Language skills, including spoken words and the unspoken ways we communicate. Some children with ASD do not speak at all; they may use communication devices, pictures, or gestures. Others can speak, but they have difficulty understanding figures of speech or words with multiple meanings. For example, hearing the leader mention that we need to "ask Jesus into our heart" or that we are "covered by the blood of Jesus" could be very confusing or frightening for a child with ASD. Or if the volunteer happens to describe a downpour by saying, "It's raining cats and dogs," he should be prepared for a huge reaction!

Repetitive behaviors or themes. Many children with ASD enjoy repeating the same activity or thinking about the same idea over and over. Sometimes this is a physical act like rocking or lining up toy vehicles; other times it is talking about the same subject or object over and over.

Sensory understanding. Children with ASD may perceive things very differently with one or more of their senses. For example, a child with a hearing sensitivity may not like loud sounds—she may cover her ears if the worship leader plays a loud song or if someone drops a book. It's also possible that a child could be undersensitive to noises, often speaking in a very loud voice or unaware that people are calling her name. A child with a vision sensitivity may look at the lights or squint. A child with differences in his tactile system may crave touch and enjoy touching certain objects, or he may dislike being touched at all.

Desire for routine. Change can be very difficult for children with ASD. A child may always choose the same chair or toy and appreciate a schedule that does not change.

Perspective-taking ability. While many of us can virtually hop into the heads of others and have a good idea of what that person might be thinking or feeling, this is very challenging for an individual with ASD. It might be difficult for a child to understand and read body language or accurately understand whether another person is happy, excited, upset, or sad.

"If I didn't see it, you didn't say it." Generally, children with ASD much prefer learning by eye than by ear. For that reason, it's important for leaders to use pictures and other visual aids in the church environment. While children will vary greatly in what they are able to learn and understand, it's important to discover the ways children best receive information and give information to others. This will set the framework for positive and helpful interactions with one another.

For continued learning and support, consider the following resources:

- *Autism and Your Church* by Barbara J. Newman (available from friendship.org)

- *Church Welcome Story* by Barbara J. Newman (clcnetwork.org)

- *Autism: A Christian Response* (Training DVD available through CLC Network; clcnetwork.org)

Autism Spectrum Disorder

Materials

- knitting or crochet project in progress
- assortment of knitted or crocheted items (sweaters, mittens, potholder, scarf)
- knitting pattern
- Bible
- picture of a baby
- paper and crayons or markers for each child
- set of keys
- a colleg-level book
- photocopies of key picture, one per child (p. 79)

Step 1

■ Show the children the knitting project. Show them how knitters can take the yarn and work with it to make a variety of beautiful things. Let the children look at the knitted or crocheted items you brought and talk about what we use them for. Let them share their amazement that a ball of yarn can turn into these items, and explain that, in order for that to happen, we need to learn how to knit. Ask if any of the children could turn that yarn into mittens. Then show the pattern that gives directions for making the project.

Step 2

■ Ask the children if they know that God is a knitter too. Read Psalm 139:13-17 and let them listen for that word. What was God knitting? Mittens? No. He was knitting people.

■ Hold up the picture of the baby. Talk about the kinds of things God used in his pattern (eye color, size and so on). Is this baby all finished growing? God puts some of the knitting pattern into a child's brain and then waits until later to do the knitting.

■ Pass out paper and have children draw their own "pattern" or self-portrait. Talk about their similarities and differences with other classmates.

■ Show the children a set of keys. What do we do with these keys? They open and start a variety of things. Say something along these lines: "Let's pretend that when we are born, God makes a set of keys for the knitting pattern. One key opens up the part of our brain that knows how to walk. Another pretend key opens the talking part. There are keys for eating and moving and reading making friends and sharing."

■ Tell the children they're going to practice using the parts of their brain that are already "open." This will give everyone a chance to stand up and move around. Ask them to move to a familiar song, perform an exercise routine, or recite a memory verse. Point out that a baby could not do those things. God has already opened up that part of their brain.

■ Then show them that some parts of our brains are still "locked up." Hold up the college-level book. Ask, "Can anyone read this book?" No. God will open up that part of their brain later when they get older. God keeps using those pretend keys. Can they think of other things that God will still open up?

■ Say, "I could talk about any one of you because God knit you together so beautifully! But today I want to tell you about our friend [name] (indicate the child). The doctors found out that

[name] has Autism Spectrum Disorder (ASD). Can you say those words? ASD means that God's knitting pattern was a little bit different for [name]. [name] has a different set of keys than you do. Some of the keys are the same, but some are different." At this point, talk about what parts of that child's brain are "unlocked"— movement, eating, and whatever this child is able to do. Some children with autism are able to read at a very early age. It may be exciting to demonstrate this to the other children. Then say, "But our friend also has some areas that are still locked up." At this point, talk about what parts of that child's brain are still locked or only partly open. Some examples may be speaking as clearly as the others, sharing, knowing how to act in church school, hearing a loud noise without jumping, and so on. Once again, make your examples specific to the child. Allow children to comment or ask questions.

- Continue the dialogue by saying, "I am so excited. It may be that while we are together, we will see God open up one part of [name]'s brain. I wonder what key that will be? God knows because God has the pattern. I believe that God has put us together in this class so that we can help [name] use one of the keys. What do you think [name] will learn to do this year? What are some ways we can help?

Step 3

- Pass out a copy of the key to each child. Have each child draw a picture or write on the key what part of the brain they hope God unlocks for their friend [name]. They may cut these out.

- Gather the children in a circle and take turns asking God to give [name] the key they just drew.

- (Option) Give each child a second copy of the key pattern and let them draw a picture or write about which part of their brain they hope God opens for them soon.

Adaptations for Younger Children

To make this presentation a bit more active, increase the number of examples of things they can already do and include some gross motor movements like hopping, clapping, singing a familiar song with motions, and the like.

Take time to delight in the keys these children already have and look forward to the many areas that God will open for them.

Note: Consider drafting a letter to families to inform them about what the class is learning about ASD. See a sample on p. 32.

Adaptations for Differing Abilities

You'll want to tailor this lesson plan to the abilities of the children in your group so every child can participate in a meaningful way. Need help? See the Activity Substitution Guide on page 73.

—Barbara J. Newman, *Autism and Your Church: Nurturing the Spiritual Growth of People with Autism Spectrum Disorder*, pp. 119-120. © 2011, Friendship Ministries. Used by permission.

Autism Spectrum Disorder

Dear Family,

"Just as a body, though one, has many parts, but all its many parts form one body, so it is with Christ" (1 Cor. 12:12). I want to take a moment to explain a little bit about the parts of the body that make up our class this year. We will learn from each person in the class, but God has made arrangements to include a child in our classroom who will be teaching us some special things. This child has autism spectrum disorder (ASD), and the family has given us permission to share the implications of that with the class and with you.

Based on our class activities, your child will be able to talk with you about ASD, but I also wanted you to have some specific information so that you'll be able to support the friendships that develop in our classroom. We want to encourage our students to play and work together, both at church and at home.

Each person in our class has different gifts and abilities, and this is true of the child with ASD as well. Most children with ASD have differences in a few areas but share many things in common with your child. The first area of difference is *language and communication*. Some children with ASD do not speak at all, while others don't understand all words the way you and I interpret them. The second area of difference is *social understanding*. Knowing how to act or interact with others can be a real challenge. Many things we think everyone should know are not always obvious to a child with ASD. A third area has to do with the *senses*—what a child hears, sees, smells, feels, or even tastes. Usually the child has one or more senses that perceive things differently than others do. Finally, a child with ASD often *focuses on one activity, topic, or movement*. Sometimes children with autism rock, flap their hands, play with one object, or talk about one topic to bring about a sense of happiness and order.

Although experts are still unsure of why children have ASD, we do know that the reason stems from the brain and areas of the brain that develop differently. I have talked with our class about ways we can help our friend learn and open up this year. I am delighted that God has given us a chance to grow in this way.

If you have any comments, questions, or concerns, please call me. I am encouraging the children to ask questions as well. Thanks for your support.

Sincerely,

Behavioral Challenges and Disorders

Note: This unit on behavioral challenges and disorders includes the following:

■ Basic Fact Sheet

■ Lesson Plan

■ Letter to Families

Please note that each child is an individual. The categories we use to describe children are helpful only in explaining general characteristics. Children with behavioral challenges and disorders vary greatly in their gifts, as well as in the significance of the impact of their areas of difference. Please be sure to contact the child's parent or guardian to obtain more specific information about the child in your group.

Behavioral Challenges and Disorders

Years ago, I went to the store to purchase bagels. Back then our small grocer offered only plain bagels, so that was easy—it was "one size fits all." Go to any bagel shop now, though, and you'll be overwhelmed by choices. Blueberry or Asiago cheese? Large or miniature? Toasted or plain? (In a way, "one size fits all" was simpler. But now I feel cheated. All those great bagels in the world, and all I had was plain.)

The category of "behavioral challenges and disorders" reminds me of today's bagel choices. Under that one heading are a wide variety of children with very different needs.

All of these kids do have a common thread that ties them together: the way they behave significantly interferes with the learning environment and with their relationships with others. Although most children have occasional outbursts and stages that are similar to those of a child with a diagnosed behavioral challenge, they are not considered to have a disability. To fit under this designation, a child's disruptive behavior must extend over a long period of time and must differ significantly from the behavior of the child's peers.

There is great variety, however, in the reasons why children are diagnosed in this way. Some children's behavior is the result of specific syndromes or psychological conditions. Some children have genetic links to others with this disability. In some cases, a child's designation is caused by his environment. Whatever the reason, these children find it hard to control themselves.

Working as a team with the child's parents is a vital part of developing a successful program for a child with a behavioral or emotional challenge. Generally, these students need high levels of structure, consistency, and patience.

One trap that is easily sprung in this category is the tendency to believe that if we make some simple changes, the children will "shape right up." Although they will likely achieve many gains through programs that encourage consistency and appropriate behavior, it's important to remember that the area of greatest need in these children is knowing how to act and get along with others.

We would never dream of expecting that a child who can't walk will suddenly be able to stroll across the room when we put the right program in place. Just as a physical therapist stretches the appropriate muscles and looks for small gains, we must be teaching behavior skills and looking for small gains. This perspective can really help teachers and classmates frame an appropriate view of the child.

Behavioral Challenges and Disorders

The behavior of children with a disability in this area can be confusing and at times scary to their peers. For this reason, I believe it is important to help peers understand the condition of behavioral challenges and disorders, even though you may find it difficult to present.

I suggest you present this material to the children by adapting the lesson plan presented in chapter 2, "The Mind That's Mine" (see pp. 17-18). Follow steps 1 and 2 of the lesson plan. Then, with the permission of the child's parent or guardian, continue the lesson as follows:

■ Tell the children you want to talk about one child in particular. You have just talked about your own strengths and weaknesses and could discuss any other child, but you want to talk about [name]. Hold up your copy of the strengths pictures as you list the strengths of the student. Talk about how this person learns by ear or eye, or talk about his or her special gifts in movement or whatever else is special about this child. Tell about the child's interests or hobbies (find out what these are from the child's parent). This can help build bridges to those with similar interests.

■ Then move into the child's areas of difficulty. Making friends is often high on that list; attention and language are also common difficulties. Explain to the children that all of our brains are different and that we want to work together to help [name] make friends this year. If there is a behavior plan in place, you may want to explain it to the class. This way they will understand why some things are set up differently for [name]. Enlist their help in befriending this child. Just as a person who can't read very well yet might need a buddy to help, this child needs some buddies to help with learning to be a good friend.

Then continue with step 3 under the lesson plan.

Adaptations for Differing Abilities

You'll want to tailor this lesson plan to the abilities of the children in your group so every child can participate in a meaningful way. Need help? See the Activity Substitution Guide on page 73.

Behavioral Challenges and Disorders

Dear Family,

Exodus 17 talks about a war between the Israelites and the Amalekites. For some reason, God set it up so that the Israelites would only be winning while Moses held up his hands. If Moses lowered his hands, the Amalekites would start winning. This became very fatiguing to Moses, so Aaron and Hur stepped in to help. Moses sat on a rock while each held one of his arms up. It took teamwork to pull off that victory.

We have a wonderful opportunity to learn more about that kind of teamwork. In our church group we have a child with a behavioral challenge or disorder who will become fatigued if we do not come alongside and help hold [his or her] arms up. Some days might require more arm-holding than others. Other days may go very smoothly.

I want to give you some of the same information I gave to your child so that as families we can support the friendships that form by allowing them to flourish in our homes and community, as well as in the church. Children with a behavioral challenge or disorder need the support of friends, so the family has given us permission to share this information with the class and with you.

For some reason, perhaps because of an illness, brain chemistry, or other factors, children who have this type of disability have difficulty practicing self-control. We want to hold up the arms of our friend by having a good behavior plan, as well as by being patient in teaching the skills that make it possible to be a good friend. We know this will take teamwork, just as it did with Moses.

I want the children in my group to be able to ask questions and to voice concerns. It's also important that you have the chance to do the same. Please feel free to call me throughout this year as we become an important support system in the life of a member of the body of Christ.

Sincerely,

Hearing Impairment

Note: This unit on hearing impairment includes the following:

■ Basic Fact Sheet

■ Lesson Plan

■ Letter to Families

Please note that each child is an individual. The categories we use to describe children are helpful only in explaining general characteristics. Children with hearing impairments vary greatly in their gifts, as well as in the significance of the impact of their areas of difference. Please be sure to contact the child's parent or guardian to obtain more specific information about the child in your group.

Hearing Impairment

Many of us know someone who has a hearing loss. Maybe you've noticed a hearing aid in someone's ear or had a conversation with a person who is unable to hear very well and who keeps asking, "What?" throughout the conversation. You may find yourself speaking more loudly to elderly people because you expect them to have a hearing loss. For a child, however, a hearing impairment can mean much more than just needing a hearing aid. Children's hearing impairments can greatly impact their speaking and language development, as well as their understanding of the environment.

Hearing impairment can be caused by different things—genetic factors, complications of pregnancy, syndromes, illnesses, or accidents. There are also different types of hearing loss:

Conductive hearing loss is caused by some complication in the outer or middle ear. Many times, surgery or hearing aids can correct this type of difference. Even so, a person with a hearing aid may need special consideration. Lots of background noise can be confusing, and certain voices may be more difficult to hear.

Sensorineural hearing loss results from damage to the inner ear or nerves located near the inner ear. This type of loss is generally more severe, and it's much more difficult to correct.

A third category of hearing impairment is called **mixed hearing loss**—a combination of conductive and sensorineural difficulties.

Although it may be helpful to understand why a person has difficulty hearing, it is probably more helpful to understand the hearing loss in terms of how loud a sound must be before he or she can hear it, as well as which pitches or frequencies are most affected. A test called an audiogram (which measures both the frequency and intensity of hearing loss) is very helpful in understanding the severity level of a hearing impairment.

For example, a person with a mild hearing impairment may find only higher and softer sounds—such as the rustling of leaves or a whispered prayer—difficult to hear. Someone with moderate hearing loss may have trouble hearing voices in certain ranges. People in the severe and profound ranges of hearing loss have trouble hearing dogs barking, lawnmowers running, telephones ringing, or horns blaring. Or they may be able to hear nothing at all. People who are unable to hear these sounds even with hearing aids or other devices are called "deaf."

Remember that a child in your group with a hearing impairment will often depend on the other senses for more information. He'll want to see your face to better understand directions, and he'll want to see the faces of the other children when he talks to them. He may need an alternate communication system like sign language or written words. He may need you to wear a special microphone when speaking so that your words are funneled directly into his hearing system. If the child is deaf, speaking may be very difficult for him. You will need to make modifications depending on the nature and severity of the hearing loss.

Finally, it is important to understand that the condition of hearing impairment has nothing to do with a person's intelligence. Although a hearing loss can occur alongside another area of disability, most children with a hearing impairment do not have an intellectual disability. These children will, however, need modifications in your church to be successful. Although it's possible that simply speaking more loudly and clearly may be helpful for a child with a hearing impairment, this could also be confusing for her. Establishing eye contact, using visual aids, establishing joint attention, and keeping down background noise are generally far more helpful communication strategies for a child with a hearing loss.

Hearing Impairment

Materials

- bell
- toy police car or fire truck with siren (or a recording of a siren)
- smoke detector
- grocery bag
- puppet with ears (can be animal or person)
- hearing aid (an audiologist may be willing to let you have an old one)
- hearing aid picture (Patterns, p. 81), one copy per child
- crayons or markers

Step 1

■ Before your session, put the bell, toy car with siren, and smoke detector into the grocery bag. When the session begins, ask the children to gather around while you play some different sounds. Keep the items in the bag hidden, and see if the children can identify the sounds you play.

■ Then talk about how these sounds warn us that something is going to happen. See if they can tell you what the sound might mean. A bell tells us _____. A siren tells us _____. A smoke detector tells us _____.

Step 2

■ Begin by saying, "Today we are going to talk about people who are not able to . . ." (at this point, begin mouthing the words with no speech). Continue to mouth words as though the children could understand you. When they ask questions or begin to complain, say, "What's the matter?" When they tell you that they can't hear your words, tell them that they have the same problem as a friend of yours who they'll meet in a moment. Tell them that your friend has a problem with his ears. Ever since he was born, he has not been able to hear the bell, the siren, or even the smoke detector. He has a hearing impairment.

■ Before you pull out the puppet, ask the children to come up with ways to tell your friend hello if he cannot hear. They may think of ideas like waving, smiling, or drawing a picture. Then pull out your puppet friend and let them say hello. You may wish to look up a few signs to teach the children so that they can talk to one another using sign language. Also talk about what you do in your group time and decide whether it would be hard or easy for the puppet to participate.

■ Then say, "We have another friend named [name] in our group (indicate the child) who has a hard time hearing—just like our puppet friend." At this point, you will need to explain more specifically about the nature and severity of the child's hearing loss. If it is mild, you can say that even though the puppet can't hear the bell, their friend [name] can hear a bell. It might, however, be hard for him to hear all of your words. If the hearing loss is severe, you can let them know that the same things that were hard for the puppet to hear are hard for their friend to hear.

■ Take some time to play a special game of "Simon Says." Play a few rounds the way the game is usually played: "Simon says . . . turn around"; "Simon says . . . clap your hands"; and so on. Then tell the children that they are going to have a chance to play Simon Says like their friend [name] plays it. As you play this time, mouth the words so the children can try to read lips; learn the signs for *jump*, *sit*, and *stand* and use those; or cover your mouth with your hand as you give directions so that the words are harder to hear. Choose the level to match the hearing loss of your student. Talk with the children about whether it was hard or easy to play that way.

Step 3

■ Give each child a copy of the picture of the hearing aid while you display a real one. Ask, "Do you know what this is? Do you know anyone who has a hearing aid? What does a hearing aid do?" Then say, "Some people wear hearing aids to help them hear a little bit better. But our friend [name] needs 'friend hearing aids.' Do you know what those are? Sometimes we might get to be a hearing aid for our friend. We might get to help [name] hear."

■ Together give some examples of what it means to be a "friend hearing aid." Talk about positive ways to help. Also talk about things for which [name] would not need friend hearing aids. It is important to help children realize that only one area of the child's ability is affected. People don't need hearing aids to see, think, eat, play, and so on.

■ Emphasize to the children that while they may be able to help their friend at times, their friend will also help them. Talk to the children about the child's gift areas so that they can also expect to receive from that friend. It's important to establish that friendship is never a one-way

street — it's a constant give and take. This friendship will be no different.

■ Provide crayons or markers and invite children to decorate the hearing aids to show a way they could help their friend this year or depict something that their friend might help them learn or understand.

■ Close by thanking God for [name] and for each one of the children and the gift of friendship.

Adaptations for Older Children

During the introduction, instead of using the bell and smoke detector, show the children a guitar. Demonstrate that a guitar works by vibrating the strings. You make lower sounds with slower vibrations and higher sounds with faster vibrations. You can play softly or loudly, depending on how hard you pull the string. Compare the guitar to the way our ears work. Our ears pick up the speed of vibrations, as well as how loud those vibrations are. This happens as the movement of small bones in our ears sends a message to our brain.

Adaptations for Differing Abilities

You'll want to tailor this lesson plan to the abilities of the children in your group so every child can participate in a meaningful way. Need help? See the Activity Substitution Guide on page 73.

Hearing Impairment

Dear Family,

"If the whole body were an eye, where would the sense of hearing be? If the whole body were an ear, where would the sense of smell be? But in fact God has placed the parts of the body, every one of them, just as he wanted them to be" (1 Cor. 12:17-18). We have a marvelous chance this year to understand this Scripture passage in a special way. Our classroom is made up of a variety of children, including one who has a hearing impairment. We hope to use this opportunity to look carefully at the gifts and needs of each member of our class and how we can work together to be complete in Jesus.

I have explained to the children about hearing impairments so that they can better understand their friend. It is our desire that the friendships we form in class will extend to the home and community. To help make that possible, I want to give you some information as well. The child's family has given us permission to share this information with the class and with you.

Most likely you know someone who has a hearing impairment. Many people function very well with a hearing aid or another adaptive device. For some people, however, the daily sounds we take for granted don't make it down the path to the brain. Sometimes the sounds stop in the outer or middle ear. If this conductive hearing loss happens, a hearing aid is often the solution. If, however, the problem is in the inner ear, where there could be some nerve damage, the sounds may never make it down the path or may be distorted. This is called a sensorineural loss. Sometimes a person has both kinds of hearing loss.

There are many different levels of severity of hearing impairment. Some people have a mild hearing loss that could make it tough to hear whispers or quiet sounds. Others are unable to hear any sounds at all. Speaking loudly to a person with a hearing loss may not be helpful. Instead, it is usually better to make eye contact, use gestures and pictures if necessary, and learn to communicate together in a common language such as sign language.

I have talked specifically with your child about the friend in our classroom who has a hearing impairment. In addition to talking about ways we can help one another, we have also talked about things our friend does not need help with. It is my desire that the children will see that "there are many parts, but one body" (1 Cor. 12:20). I am encouraging the children to ask questions. Please feel free to do the same.

Sincerely,

Intellectual Disability

Note: This unit on intellectual disability includes the following:

■ Basic Fact Sheet

■ Lesson Plan

■ Letter to Families

Please note that each child is an individual. The categories we use to describe children are helpful only in explaining general characteristics. Children with intellectual disabilities vary greatly in their gifts, as well as in the impact of their areas of difference. Please be sure to contact the child's parent or guardian to obtain more specific information about the child in your group.

Intellectual Disability

remember attending a girls' club at my church when I was a child. One year, when the leader announced a special Christmas caroling project, I was in for a surprise. I'd been expecting our usual visit to the local nursing home, where the thermostat was always set way too high for my comfort. Not this time. Instead of sweating in those halls again, we'd be singing at a place called Children's Retreat—an institution for children with intellectual disabilities. My internal thermostat went way up with fear and apprehension. I could only imagine what that place would be like.

I believe that fear-filled reaction was far more typical several years ago, when persons with intellectual disabilities were routinely housed in large institutions and special schools. Since the laws governing how our society understands and interacts with those with intellectual disabilities have changed, and communities are required to provide educational and housing options within local schools and neighborhoods, we are far more likely to have contact with persons who have an intellectual disability.

A child is considered to have an intellectual disability based on two factors. The first is having an IQ score below 70. The second is having differences in adaptive behavior. This means that the lower IQ negatively impacts a child's ability to function in everyday situations.

Within this category, the children's ability level varies widely. Children who are impacted in a milder way have an IQ score between 55 and 70. They have the ability to learn some reading and math skills. It takes these children longer to master the limited material, but they have the potential to learn

alongside the other children in the class. As they get older, the gap gets wider. This makes early childhood settings exciting places for inclusion.

Children with an IQ score between 40 and 55 are considered to have a moderate level of intellectual disability. These children may be able to learn to read select words and may be trained to acquire some specific work skills. Interaction with typical peers allows these children to understand more clearly how to communicate and how to get along with others. These are critical skills to learn as children prepare for their future in society.

Children with an IQ score below 40 fall in the severe range of intellectual disability. Their ability to work within a typical group setting varies greatly from individual to individual. The group's leader will most likely require an extra volunteer or buddy in the room to help meet the needs of this child. If a child with an intellectual disability in your group falls into this category, I encourage you to use the "Severe Disability" section of chapter 5 to help your group best understand this friend.

Intellectual disabilities are most often caused by chromosomal differences. Other causes of intellectual disability include complications of pregnancy, maternal drug use, and lack of oxygen at birth.

The most common and easily identified genetic cause is Down syndrome. Children with Down syndrome have 47 chromosomes instead of 46. This produces a predictable order of development noticeable in the absence of nose bridges, unique eye positioning, heightened health difficulties, and a level of intellectual disability.

While you will notice a difference in the child's thinking and learning, make sure to remember that those things are only one part of the child. The child is an imagebearer of God, uniquely crafted by him and gifted in such a way that the child's presence will teach others in the group. As you accommodate for the child's areas of difference with adapted learning materials or communication supports, make sure you also find ways to highlight the child's personality, talents, gifts, loves, and presence.

Finally, remember that children with intellectual disabilities need to be treated based on their actual age, not on their mental age. It is an insult to treat an adult or older child with an intellectual disability like a very young child. If a child is seven, then you should treat her like others who are seven. Of course, you'll need to modify academic instruction, but you should hold high expectations in the areas of social interaction and behavior. In other words, simplify the material, not your interactions. Don't use the tone of voice or body language you would use with a much younger child. Always respect the dignity of people with disabilities.

Intellectual Disability

Materials

- *The Very Hungry Caterpillar* by Eric Carle
- pictures of butterflies
- set of interlocking blocks (Lego® or Duplo® blocks)
- paper and scissors
- paint and paintbrushes
- small picture of each child in the group (take your own photos beforehand, or ask parents to send them in)
- *Be Good to Eddie Lee* by Virginia Fleming (optional)

Step 1

■ Read aloud Eric Carle's classic picture book *The Very Hungry Caterpillar*. Then talk with the children about how caterpillars turn into butterflies. Show your collection of butterfly pictures. Let the children compare how they differ in color, size, shape, and so on.

Step 2

■ Explain that, like butterflies, children are different too. Note some of the differences among the children in your class.

■ Use your Lego® or Duplo® blocks to begin building a tower that everyone can see. Meanwhile, hold a discussion along these lines: "When God was building you—before you were even born—he knew that Shelley would have green eyes (pull out green block) and Tim would have brown hair (add a brown block to green one) and James would have five fingers on each hand" (add five blocks). Continue this until you have a fairly large tower.

■ Then say, "God used lots of different building blocks to make each one of you a special tower. Some of the blocks he used are the same—like the way David and Abby both have a block for blue eyes. Some of the blocks God used only for one person. I want to tell you about a special block that only our friend [name] has in this class."

■ At this point, you will need to be specific about the child's intellectual disability. If the child has Down syndrome, designate a color and say that that block is called Down syndrome. If the disability has no specific cause or is caused by factors that are too difficult for the children to understand, simply label the block "intellectual disability." Add that block to the tower and note that only [name] has this block.

■ If the child has Down syndrome, say something like the following. If not, go on to the next bullet. "When God puts our building blocks together, he uses something called chromosomes. Most people have forty-six chromosomes, but [name] has forty-seven. Forty-seven means that some things are easy for [name] and some are harder." You could illustrate by asking the child to demonstrate his flexibility. Generally, children with Down syndrome can touch their nose to the ground while seated cross-legged on the floor. Let the other children try. They will be amazed. Proceed to tell about the things this child enjoys—music, throwing balls, or being with friends. Continue by saying, "People with forty-seven chromosomes also have a hard time with a few things." You can point out to the children that having a tongue with weaker muscles makes it more difficult to speak. You may also say that it can be more difficult to learn to read or learn about numbers. Make this specific to the child in your group.

- If the child has an intellectual disability that is not Down syndrome, say something like the following: "When people have an intellectual disability block in their tower, there are many things they like to do, but a few things are harder for them." Let the children know what their classmate likes to do. Some areas to investigate are music, ball games, favorite restaurants, and so on. Then talk to the children about some things that are more difficult for the child because of the intellectual disability block: things like speaking, learning to read, motor skills, and so on. Again, you'll want to make sure these are specific to the child in your group.

- Using one of your butterfly pictures, cut out a small hole where the head should be. Insert a picture of the child who has an intellectual disability. (You'll want to prepare this ahead of time.) Remind the children of the story *The Very Hungry Caterpillar* you read together earlier. Tell the children you have a surprise butterfly for them to see. God has painted it in a special way. Show them the picture and say, "[Name] is turning into a beautiful butterfly."

Step 3

- Tell the children that you believe God is turning each one of them into a beautiful butterfly too. Each one is different and special because each has a different tower of blocks. Some may have blocks for being a fast runner, others for drawing pictures, others for intellectual disability, others for being tall, and so on.

- Distribute paper, scissors, paintbrushes, and paint to the children, and then demonstrate how to fold the paper in half and cut out a butterfly. Let children paint their own butterfly, and insert their picture where a head should be. Close in a prayer of thanks for each one of God's butterflies.

- (Optional) Read the book *Be Good to Eddie Lee* by Virginia Fleming and talk about friends. Who was a good friend in the book? Who was not?

Adaptations for Younger Children

As you begin your discussion, talk about how children are different, just like butterflies are different. Take turns covering each child with a blanket. Let each pop out like a butterfly and note how beautifully unique each child is.

Adaptations for Older Children

Instead of using paint for the butterflies, encourage children to draw a butterfly and fill its outline with symbols of things that make them unique creations of God. Show them how to insert their picture where the butterfly's head should be. Thank God for each one.

Adaptations for Differing Abilities

You'll want to tailor this lesson plan to the abilities of the children in your group so every child can participate in a meaningful way. Need help? See the Activity Substitution Guide on page 73.

Intellectual Disability

Dear Family,

We plan to praise God in our class, and I want to tell you about a special opportunity we have for praising God this year. The Bible says, "Accept one another, then, just as Christ accepted you, in order to bring praise to God" (Rom. 15:7). How exciting that we praise God by accepting one another!

We will have many chances to show our acceptance to each person in the class. In order to do this in the best possible way, I have talked with the children about a member of our class who has an intellectual disability. Sometimes it's easier to accept a person when we understand a bit more about his or her differences. In order to help extend this acceptance beyond the church and into our homes, I want you to have some specific information about intellectual disabilities as well. The child's family has given us permission to share this information with the class and with you.

A child with an intellectual disability will have many of the same interests as your child. There are differences, however, in the speed and quantity of what the child will learn. Children with intellectual disabilities take longer to learn to read, for example. Some children may be able to master only those words we see every day, like "restroom" or "exit." In any case, we learn best from our peers. Therefore, your child will be a wonderful peer model for things like how to speak, how to act, and how to be a friend. Likewise, your child will also have the benefit of being in community with someone who will undoubtedly impact your child's life in many positive ways.

I will be talking very specifically with the group about being a friend—not a mother or father—to our classmate. We know that Christ's attitude toward us is filled with unconditional love, as well as high expectations. This is what we hope to offer our friend, as well as each member of our classroom.

If you have any questions, please feel free to contact me. We want the children to talk openly this year about intellectual disabilities, and I ask the same of you.

Sincerely,

Physical Disability

Note: This unit on physical disability includes the following:

- Basic Fact Sheet

- Lesson Plan

- Letter to Families

Please note that each child is an individual. The categories we use to describe children are helpful only in explaining general characteristics. Children with physical disabilities vary greatly in their gifts, as well as in the impact of some of their areas of difference. Please be sure to contact the child's parent or guardian to obtain more specific information about the child in your group.

Physical Disability

Some types of physical disability greatly impact a child's ability to be involved in a group setting. If this is the case, refer to the section of chapter 5 on severe disabilities. Additional forms of physical disability include medical conditions such as mild cerebral palsy, epilepsy, or asthma. Other physical disabilities may result from a genetic condition, disease, or accident. It is not my intention here to try to list every possibility. However, I do want to give you a few suggestions for working with children with physical disabilities in your church setting.

Depending on the cause and nature of the physical disability, a child may need some learning and environment modifications. Contact the child's parent or guardian to find out the best way to help her. Some children may need to be pushed to perform up to their potential; others may need you to intervene if they are trying too hard to keep up with the rest of the group. Some children may have diet and activity restrictions; others may need physical modifications to enable them to participate in group activities.

With some children, there may be very specific instructions for you to follow in terms of emergency procedures, supports for eating or using the bathroom, or positioning and using specialized equipment. It's important for these instructions to be clearly communicated to all leaders and volunteers who interact with the child. Having printed instructions and a training session often allows church workers to feel empowered and comfortable when interacting with a child whose physical disability may necessitate certain procedures or emergency interventions. If a child has a seizure disorder, for example, it's important for all leaders to know exactly what to expect and how to respond if a seizure happens during church hours. Arming leaders with specific information is important for the child's safety, as well as the leaders' confidence.

It's important to emphasize that our bodies are not the whole of our person. That's as true for children with a physical disability as it is for all other children. The disability is one small part of who the child is. Your job as a leader is to draw on the child's strengths and areas of growth, while accommodating the areas needing support. Remember that God looks at our heart, not our outward appearance (1 Sam. 16:7).

Physical Disability

Some disabilities are more noticeable than others. A child in a wheelchair, for example, will create more of a stir in your group than a child who walks with a slight limp because one leg is shorter than the other. Both are physical disabilities. But the children in your class may need information about the disability in one case and not in another. Use your judgment and communicate with the child's parents to decide whether the group would benefit from learning more about that child and his or her equipment or emergency plan.

Consider some of these areas as you decide what you may want peers to know:

- **Does the child have any specialized equipment?** If so, some peers will shy away from or inappropriately touch or ask about the equipment. Sometimes it can be helpful to talk with peers, for example, about a wheelchair being that individual's legs and something we don't touch without permission from that person. Explaining about a child's leg braces or walker and the function they serve can help demystify those items and better allow children to connect with the friend who happens to use those items.

- **Can children try out any of the needed equipment?** If the friend uses canes, a walker, a wheelchair, a specialized chair, or specialized scissors or pencils, friends often benefit from having a chance to try those items out. This takes the mystery out of the equipment and may allow interactions to happen in a more typical fashion. Make sure you obtain permission from the child and the child's parents if you'd like to allow children to investigate these items.

- **Would the peers be impacted if an emergency were to happen?** Sometimes it's necessary to have an emergency response plan that includes the other children. If peers will be asked to vacate an area or to get some adult help, it's important for them to know and practice that plan. Explaining more about the child's potential emergency and how to respond can often create an atmosphere of understanding and confidence, should something occur during church time. If peers are part of the plan, they certainly need to be informed and trained.

- **Does the child have a story that parents or the child would like to share?** Some parents have even created a book about their child with a disability so that others can learn his or her story. Learning about the child's history and situation often opens new doors of understanding and friendship. God's hand in any one of our lives is amazing, and this is one way of giving peers a chance to see God's touch in the life of a friend.

LETTER TO FAMILIES
Physical Disability

Dear Family,

Our group at church is filled with such a variety of children, each with differing areas of gifts and areas of need. As part of celebrating each child in our group, I spent some time today delighting in one of our friends. We enjoyed learning about some things that are easy for our friend and other areas that are more difficult. This friend happens to have a physical disability. The child's family has given us permission to share this information with the class and with you.

A child with a physical disability may need specialized equipment, procedures, or understanding. We wanted to empower your child to best understand that disability so that the children could focus on being friends with one another, as opposed to wondering about the physical disability. Feel free to ask your child about our discussion so that you will also understand what might be helpful for this friend. It's my hope that the friendships extend beyond the church walls, so I also want to equip you to support friendship opportunities that could happen in your home or community.

It's such a delight to have a group filled with diversity. Just as King David clearly demonstrated that Jonathan's son, Mephibosheth, who had a physical disability, was an honored and welcome participant at each meal at the king's table, we have the chance to demonstrate to our group that same idea this year. Mephibosheth's presence was based on whose son he was, and we also have the chance to delight in being the sons and daughters of God, coming together with all of our strengths and all of our weaknesses. As God holds his arms open to each one of us, may we extend our arms of friendship to one another as well.

Feel free to let me know if you have any additional questions.

Sincerely,

Visual Impairment

Note: This unit on visual impairment includes the following:

■ Basic Fact Sheet

■ Lesson Plan

■ Letter to Families

Please note that each child is an individual. The categories we use to describe children are helpful only in explaining general characteristics. Children with visual impairments vary greatly in their gifts, as well as in the impact of some of their areas of difference. Please be sure to contact the child's parent or guardian to obtain more specific information about the child in your group.

Visual Impairment

Many of us can relate to this particular category personally. We all know someone who wears glasses or contact lenses. Maybe we wear them ourselves. Lots of people have a pair of prescription glasses tucked away in their car or purse. These corrective lenses tell us that we have differences in our vision. In most cases, life goes on beautifully with a little help from an optometrist. For some of us, however, impaired vision turns into a visual impairment.

The term *visual impairment* is used when a person has difficulty with everyday tasks even with the help of corrective glasses or equipment. A visual impairment can range from mild to severe. On the mild end of the spectrum, a child may need large-print editions of books or different lighting or equipment to see better. On the more severe end, a child may be considered totally blind and need to acquire skills in Braille and in navigating with a cane. In either case, you'll need to make some modifications to your group for the child with a visual impairment.

The causes of visual impairments are numerous. Some people are blind from birth. Others lose vision as a result of accidents or eye injuries. Difficulty seeing can be caused by developmental factors or medical conditions of the eye. You'll want to find out the exact cause and nature of your child's vision loss from a parent or guardian.

Children who have never been able to see have no mental images to associate with concepts like colors or other descriptive adjectives. Those who have gradually lost sight over a period of time may have a strong memory of these images. For that reason it is important for you to know the age of onset of the visual impairment in order to understand what the child understands.

If the child in your class has a mild vision impairment, this material may not be helpful. If, however, he has a more severe vision problem, developing sensitivity in the other children is important. The child with the disability will often depend heavily on his other senses to operate in the church setting. The other children will need to be aware of the importance of creating a safe environment. They'll also need a firm understanding of the fact that having a visual impairment does not mean that the child also has an intellectual disability. Although some children do have more than one area of disability, most children with a visual impairment can learn as well as any other child in the classroom, given the correct modifications.

Visual Impairment

Materials

- CD recording of environmental sounds: water running, someone laughing, toilet flushing, phone ringing, and so on. (Purchase these at a teacher's store, find online, or record your own.)
- a variety of objects to touch that are easily identifiable: cotton ball, rubber band, cup, and so on
- paper or cloth bag
- picture of eyes, ears, and fingers (Patterns, p. 83)
- name card for each child
- notecards
- waxed paper
- glasses (Patterns, p. 82), photocopied on cardstock
- crayons or markers
- scissors

Step 1

■ Invite the children to play a game of "I Spy." ("I spy with my little eye something that is . . ." round, orange, big, and so on.) The others must try to guess what you see.

■ Then try a new round by changing it to "I hear with my little ear something that is . . ." loud, soft, musical, and so on. Then play the sound from the recording. See if the children can guess the sound.

■ The final round of this game will be "I touch with my little hand something that is . . ." soft, bumpy, small, and so on. Let children touch one of the objects you collected by putting it in a bag so they cannot see it. Can they guess what it is?

Step 2

■ Cut apart and display the pictures of the eyes, ears, and fingers. Talk about the "I Spy" games you just played. Which one was easiest for them? Let them vote by placing their name card under the eyes, ears, or fingers picture.

■ Then talk about some of the different things God created that children like to see. Give each child an index card. Have them draw or write the name of something they like to see and place it under the eye picture. Do the same for things they like to hear and touch.

■ Say, "I am so thankful for all of these things that God made. I love animals like dogs because God lets me see them run, hear them bark, and feel their soft fur." Ask the children if they can come up with another example of something we can see, hear, and touch. Then say, "That's especially important for our friend [name]. It was hard for [name] to play 'I Spy,' but it was easy for her to play 'I Hear' and 'I Touch.' It would be hard for [name] to see a dog, but she can hear it bark and touch its soft fur. Do you know why that is?"

■ As children come up with answers, share some information with them about your student who has a visual impairment. (She may wish to talk about it too.) What is this person able to see? Has she always had a visual impairment? Why does she have trouble seeing?

- Give each child a piece of waxed paper to hold over his or her eyes. Encourage them to say how many fingers you are holding up or look at a picture on the wall. Invite them to imagine what it would be like if this were the way their eyes worked all the time. Would it be easy to play baseball? What about singing a song? Talk about a variety of things you do in your classroom and decide what would be hard and what would be easy if you had a visual impairment.

Step 3

- If you wear glasses, show them to the kids; if you don't, borrow someone's reading glasses before class. Say, "Sometimes people wear glasses to help them see. But our friend [name] might need 'friend glasses.' Do you know what those are? Sometimes we might have a chance to be glasses for our friend [name]. We might have to help her see."

- Brainstorm with the children to come up with some examples of being "friend glasses." Talk about positive ways to help.

- Then talk about things for which [name] does not need "friend glasses." It is equally important to help the children realize that only one of the child's senses is affected. People don't need glasses to hear, speak, think, eat, and so on.

- It's also important for the children to know that friends learn from one another. While they may be helping the friend with the visual impairment one week, that friend might have an idea or answer to help them the next week.

- Distribute crayons or markers, along with cardstock glasses for children to cut out and/or decorate.

- Close by thanking God for [name] and for each one of the children and the friendships they can have with one another.

Adaptations for Older Children

Instead of using the phrase "I spy with my little eye something that is . . ." use "I see something that is . . ." or "I hear something that is. . . ."

Adaptations for Differing Abilities

You'll want to tailor this lesson plan to the abilities of the children in your group so every child can participate in a meaningful way. Need help? See the Activity Substitution Guide on page 73.

Visual Impairment

Dear Family,

The Bible records many stories of Jesus reaching out to someone who could not see and healing him. This year, God is allowing your child to reach out and touch someone who has a visual impairment, and we also know this child will be reaching out and touching the life of your child in return.

We have talked as a class about our friend who has a visual impairment. Please ask your child to tell you about our "I Spy" games. In order to make this year go smoothly and to allow your child's friendship to extend out of our church and into your home, I want to give you some information about visual impairments too. The child's family has given us permission to share this information with the class and with you.

Although anyone who needs to wear glasses or contact lenses has impaired vision, most of us are able to fully participate in daily living without any more assistance than our corrective lenses provide. If, however, the vision problem did impact our daily routine (even with glasses), then we would be considered to be visually impaired. Some children with a visual impairment are completely unable to see; others have limited vision. Vision impairments can be the result of an eye problem from birth, an accident, or a condition that develops as the child grows. Some children benefit from large print or special lighting; others read Braille and use a cane to move around.

The children in this group have talked very specifically about the gifts and needs of their friend. Your child knows how to reach out to help [him or her] in ways that recognize that our friend only has difficulty seeing—not hearing or thinking or learning. Although we will be careful to set up our room in a safe way or guide our friend when needed, [he or she] is a member of our class just as the other children are.

If you have any questions, please feel free to give me a call. We are excited about this chance to be with one another as friends this year.

Sincerely,

CHAPTER 5
Additional Areas of Disability

Disabilities Often Diagnosed during the School Years

Severe and/or Multiple Disabilities

Disabilities Often Diagnosed during the School Years

Note: This unit includes the following:

■ Basic Fact Sheet—Attention Deficit/ Hyperactivity Disorder

■ Basic Fact Sheet—Learning Disabilities

■ Basic Fact Sheet—Speech and Language Disorders

■ Suggestions for Presenting Information to Children on Disabilities Often Diagnosed during the School Years

Leaders may use this material in connection with the lesson plan "The Mind That's Mine" (pp. 17-18) to present information on any of the above disabilities to students as needed.

Attention Deficit/Hyperactivity Disorder

When you're at church, have you ever sat right behind a family where one child seemed out of control? It's tempting to think that if only the parents would be more firm, the child would shape right up. Unfortunately, that judgment is routinely passed on families with children who are diagnosed with attention deficit/hyperactivity disorder (AD/HD). This disability is fairly common among adults as well as children. Children, however, often find themselves in places where it's difficult to escape the demands of paying attention and "sitting still."

There are basically three types of attention disorders: impulsive, inattentive, and combined. Children with AD/HD impulsive type are generally very active, and impulsive in actions and thoughts. When describing this child, we sometimes reference the "ready, fire, aim" approach to life. Children with AD/HD inattentive type have a mind that often drifts from the topic at hand, so they find themselves daydreaming and off topic. When the church school volunteer is talking about one of the miracles of Jesus, this child may be smiling at the leader and thinking about the vacation he took last summer. AD/HD combined type describes children who have both impulsivity and inattention.

The cause of AD/HD is neurological. The neurotransmitter chemical responsible for attention is not doing its job. This chemical should lie in the synapse between neurons in the brain. If there is not enough of this chemical, or if it is not in the synapse, the child will have difficulty concentrating. In many cases, medication to help the neurotransmitter do the job correctly can bring relief from the symptoms for the length of time the medication is in the body. Most medications are effective for between four and twelve hours, and then the symptoms of AD/HD return until the next medication dose. Some children take medication only during school hours, so evening church meetings and weekend events can be a challenge for their attention systems.

If you have a child or children in your group with attention disorders, you'll find it helpful to establish an environment where children experience consistent expectations and consequences. You'll also want to use visual and auditory cues to direct their attention. Many of these children will go on to choose professions where the demands of attention fit with their often creative, fast-moving brains. As a leader, your job is to nurture and support them in the classroom setting—an environment they find difficult.

Children with AD/HD generally have typical intellectual functioning, and often they have great strengths to contribute. It's important for these children to be able to use their gifts in church settings. No one wants to do what is difficult for them all day long. Encouraging the use of gifts of movement, artistic expression, drama, poetry, and other interests gives them something to look forward to in the church setting.

The level of severity varies greatly in children with AD/HD. Some children need only minor modifications in a structured setting; others will need much support and planning. Always remember that this area of disability has a biological cause—and temper your responses with this knowledge. We would never dream of telling a child with diabetes that if she simply produces more insulin, we'll reward her with a sticker. That's impossible for her. Yet we often expect children with AD/HD to miraculously produce more neurotransmitters for attention when we offer them rewards or punishments.

While we need to have appropriate expectations, consistent leaders who focus on the gifts this child brings to the environment will often release him or her to have a wonderful church experience.

Learning Disabilities

This term covers a very broad category of children who have a typical intelligence level but who are unable to perform at that level for a variety of reasons. For example, a child's scores on a test may predict that he should do well in reading based on his intellectual abilities. But for some reason he is not able to perform at the expected level.

Children may have a learning disability in one or more areas. Typically, these areas include reading, math, writing, reasoning, organization, or spoken language skills. You'll need to find out what specific area is difficult for the child in your group.

This book cannot give you specific strategies for dealing with each situation. It's important, however, to be sensitive to the child's needs. For example, if she has difficulty reading aloud, consider assigning her a reading buddy, and don't expect her to read aloud unless she's doing a choral reading with others or has had a chance to prepare and practice ahead of time. If you assign the class a long written assignment, perhaps you'll want to modify your expectations for this child. He may be able to work on the assignment at home or as a part of a small group. Use his strengths to build his confidence and to help other students understand his contributions to your class. Be flexible in the way you present information and in what you expect from children in response.

During his life on earth, Jesus showed that he was a master at understanding each individual. He adjusted his speech, his expectations, his body language, and his intervention based on who that person was and what she needed. As we seek to follow Jesus, we can trust him to give us that insight into our children.

Speech and Language Disorders

The largest category of children in special education is those who have speech and language disorders. For some children, having a speech disorder simply means they need to work on a few letter sounds. Others may not be able to speak at all; they may communicate with sign language or with a computerized device. Generally, children with a severe language disorder also have another type of disability, such as an intellectual disability. They may also have speech patterns and skills that have changed dramatically through accident or disease. For the most part, however, children in this category have mild needs that require sensitivity on the part of the leader and peers. Be aware that people with speech and language disorders often understand more than they can express.

Depending on the needs of the child, you will need to be flexible in the way you present your material, as well as in how you expect the child to respond. For example, if a child's vocabulary is weak, you can present a concept visually by showing a picture or object. You'll want to provide options for responding other than speaking. You may need to equip your classroom with picture boards or other objects a child can point to. Consider allowing a child who stutters to make a visual presentation as opposed to a verbal report. The idea is to be flexible and supportive of the child's particular speech and language needs.

The Old Testament gives us a wonderful example of how a man with a speech disorder was used by God for a special task. Moses was hesitant to do God's will because of his disorder: "'I have never been eloquent, neither in the past nor since you have spoken to your servant. I am slow of speech and tongue.' The Lord said to him, 'Who gave human beings their mouths? . . . Is it not I, the LORD? Now go; I will help you speak and will teach you what to say'" (Ex. 4:10-12).

God did not allow a speech difference to stand in the way of his appointed leader. God provided for his needs and encouraged him to accept the challenge. What an awesome model for us to follow!

Suggestions for Presenting Information to Children on Disabilities Often Diagnosed during the School Years

Some disabilities are more noticeable than others. A child who is unable to use spoken language, for example, will create more questions in your group than a child who might find it difficult to pronounce the letter "r." Both are speech and language disorders. But the children in your group may need information about the disability in one case and not in the other.

Use your judgment and communicate with the child's parents to decide whether the peers would best understand that friend with some information about the area of disability. Be sensitive to the comments and questions of the other children, as well as to the comfort level of the child with the disability.

If you decide that your group will benefit from the information, I suggest you follow the lesson plan in "The Mind That's Mine" (pp. 17-18). After presenting your own strengths and weaknesses in step 2, tell the children that you are going to be talking about one other member of your class. First talk to the children about the child's strengths. After that, discuss the area of weakness. Then continue with step 3, in which the children detail their own strengths and weaknesses. As questions or comments arise throughout the year, you can refer back to this activity. You'll want to stress that we all have strengths and weaknesses because of our unique brain patterns.

Severe and/or Multiple Disabilities

Note: This unit on severe impairment includes the following:

- Basic Fact Sheet

- Lesson Plan

- Letter to Families

Please note that each child is an individual. The categories we use to describe children are helpful only in explaining general characteristics. Children with severe and/or multiple disabilities vary greatly in their gifts, as well as in the impact of their areas of difference. Please be sure to contact the child's parent or guardian to obtain more specific information about the child in your group.

BASIC FACT SHEET
Severe and/or Multiple Disabilities

Some children are born with (or experience as the result of an accident or disease) more than one area of disability. Others are diagnosed with a single disability, but there is a significant impact on the child. Incorporating a child with severe and/or multiple disabilities into your group will require good planning, teamwork, and much understanding on the part of all involved.

I won't list all the possible areas of severe disability here. Instead I will mention some common characteristics these children may have.

- First of all, you can expect limited speech. Often children will have some type of alternate speech system, such as a few basic signs or a board with pictures so they can point to what they need.

- Many children with severe disabilities also have difficulty moving around physically. Some may use a wheelchair or need special devices or braces.

- Children with severe and/or multiple disabilities will also often need repeated practice on skills. In many cases they are able to perform a task in one environment without being able to translate it to a new environment. For example, a child may be able to wave hello at home but will need to be taught to wave hello at church as well.

- Finally, the child will need support in all areas of life—working, playing, home life, school life, and church life.

I encourage you to thoroughly research the gifts and needs of your child. Remember that it is entirely possible for a child to be able to move only one body part and yet have completely typical intelligence. It is also possible for a child to have a perfectly functioning body and yet have a severe intellectual disability that will never allow him to understand more than an infant can understand. Be sure to find out about any important medical or physical conditions requiring tube feeding, help with personal care, or special seating equipment and positions.

Teaching children with severe and/or multiple disabilities is both a great challenge and a great blessing. Even after teaching children with intellectual disabilities for many years, it was eye-opening for me to enter a school reserved for children with severe disabilities. I looked around at the children and could only ask God, "Why? What is the purpose? Where is your miraculous touch for these children?"

I can't answer those questions. But I do know that children with severe disabilities bear God's image and have something significant to teach us and our communities. From them I have learned more about prayer and about bringing people I love constantly before God. I have learned compassion. I have learned that God forms relationships with all kinds of people. Most of all, I have learned to long for the day when we will all be clothed with our new bodies, a time when "there will be no more death or mourning or crying or pain" (Rev. 21:4). I trust you will learn from them too.

LESSON PLAN
Severe and/or Multiple Disabilities

Materials

- paper or posterboard
- pencils, crayons or markers, scissors, glue sticks
- personal items, such as photos of each child and his or her family, baby pictures, pictures of things each child especially likes, and so on. (You will have to contact each family ahead of time to assemble these supplies.)
- ball of twine
- strips of construction paper, 1 inch by 8 inches (or 3 cm by 20 cm). However many children are in your group, you'll need that many strips per child. So if there are ten children, you'll need 100 strips. Use a paper cutter to make strips quickly.

Step 1

■ Distribute large sheets of paper or posterboard, scissors, glue, pencils, and crayons or markers. Invite each child to create a poster titled "All about Me." Invite them to include the personal items they brought along and to draw on the poster some of their favorite things, things they like to do, and other things that make them who they are. If your group includes a child with a severe disability who will have difficulty making a poster, help that child create a poster. Alternately, consider asking the child's parent or guardian to join the group to assemble the collage.

Step 2

■ Let children take turns showing their completed posters to the whole group. Comment that everyone here has a family, but the families are different. Everyone here was a baby, but each one looked different. Everyone has things they

like to do, but those things are different from one child to another. If the child with the disability is unable to present her poster to the group, you or the parent or guardian can present the poster.

■ When all the posters have been admired by the group, say something like this: "Each one of you is a very special person. I could talk about any one of you, but today I want to tell you a little bit about our friend [name]. [Name] has a poster like you do, because there are many things that are the same. But [name] also has some things that are different. In order to help you be better friends, I want to tell you about them." Proceed to explain about the child's specific disability. You may wish to refer to the chapter on specific disabilities to help gather the information you need. If the child has a vision impairment, talk about that. If she has an intellectual disability, talk about that. If he uses a wheelchair, let the children check it out. If he uses sign language, teach the sign for "Hello" and a few other signs to the other children. If she uses a communication board, let them see it and try it.

■ Then ask the children some questions designed to help them understand their classmate better. Get their opinions and, if necessary, gently steer them to the correct answer. For example, "Is it OK to touch [name]?" "Is it OK to talk to [name]?" "Will [name] be able to play with toys?" "What does it mean when [name] makes those noises?" Often children with severe disabilities can seem a bit scary to their classmates. Make sure you talk about that. As you talk about it, the children will learn to feel comfortable as well.

- Remember to model for the children how to touch and talk to the child with the disability. Is there a game the children could play with that child? If so, teach it to the group.

Step 3

- Make a circle and hold hands with the group. Sit on the floor and hand the ball of twine to one group member. The child should say the name of any person in the group and toss the twine to him or her. With each toss, have the child keep holding the string so that it begins to form a web tying the children together. If a child with a severe disability is unable to throw or catch the twine, make sure she is connected to the web. Help her grasp the twine if possible, or drape the twine across her lap before you pass it to the next person. When all the children are connected with this web, show them that if even one person lets go, the web is not as strong. We need to all be a part of this group. Mention each child by name and say, "You are all important people in God's family and in this group."

- Give each child as many strips of construction paper as there are children in your group (if there are ten children, give them each ten strips). Ask them to write their name on each of the strips. When everyone has finished, let the kids take turns giving their name strips to each of their classmates. When they all have a set of strips with everyone's names, they can staple or glue the strips together to form a chain. Show them how to link the ends of their chain into a circle to show the unity of the group. If the child with a severe disability will have difficulty doing this activity, help out in any way you can.

Adaptations for Older Children

Instead of making a poster in step 1, have each child work on a pennant describing one of the most awesome creations God has ever made—him- or herself. Use the suggested items for the poster or encourage the children to come up with their own ideas.

Adaptations for Differing Abilities

You'll want to tailor this lesson plan to the abilities of the children in your group so every child can participate in a meaningful way. Need help? See the Activity Substitution Guide on page 73.

Severe and/or Multiple Disabilities

Dear Family,

"Consequently, you are no longer foreigners and strangers, but fellow citizens with God's people and also members of his household, built on the foundation of the apostles and prophets, with Christ Jesus himself as the chief cornerstone. In him the whole building is joined together and rises to become a holy temple in the Lord" (Eph. 2:19-20).

Years ago, one of our classmates would have felt like a foreigner and a stranger in our group. Years ago, the child in our group who has a disability would have been sent to live in an institution, cut off from family and friends. I'm thankful that we now understand a bit more about what it means to "join all of the pieces of the temple together." We want our group to be a place where each person is recognized as a part of the temple of God.

In order to help us act as one building joined together by Jesus, I have given the children some information about our friend with a disability. I want to give you some information as well, so that the bonds that are formed in our group can extend to our homes and community. The child's family has given us permission to share this information with the class and with you.

Most often, a child with a severe disability or more than one area of disability will need help completing tasks at home, at school, in church, and in the community. This child will frequently have difficulty in communicating, as well as in physically getting around. Although some children who have many physical needs have typical intellectual functioning, it is often the case that a child with a severe disability will have difficulty understanding many concepts and tasks.

One thing we can all understand, however, is the love and acceptance shown us by friends. For this reason, I have talked with your child about how to touch, communicate, and play with our friend. I am thankful we have the opportunity to be together this year and learn from one another.

I have encouraged the children to ask questions, and I ask you to feel free to do the same.

Sincerely,

CHAPTER 6

Lesson Plan for Middle School and High School

While many of the lesson plans in this book can be adapted to reach different age groups, this lesson is especially designed to help older children and teens value all people, including those with disabilities, as dearly loved children of God.

In parts of this lesson, leaders may want to insert information specific to the areas of disability that affect people in the group or classroom. This lesson can also be used as a general way to build community within a church youth group or education setting for older children and teens.

Materials:

- empty table
- thick black or blue marker
- several pieces of blank paper
- writing paper and pens or pencils for each member of the group
- set of self-stick labels (similar to address labels for envelopes) for each person. Make sure you have a few extra sets of labels for the group activity. Before class, use a printer to print the following words (one per label) on each set: *important, honored, member of the body of Christ, indispensable, dearly loved child of God, salt and light of the world, handcrafted by God, forgiven, gifted, Mine.*
- blank piece of posterboard taped to the wall (you may need more than one piece of posterboard if your group is large)
- colored markers for writing names
- camera (optional)

Step 1

- Set up an empty table in the middle of the room. Since many kids this age are looking for employment, have them imagine with you that each of them now works at the local department store. For one of their first jobs, they will be asked to fill a table with clearance items to make room for new merchandise. It's their job to decide which items in the imaginary store should be sold at clearance prices.

- Ask the kids, "As you walk through the store, what characteristics will you look for as you decide what things to sell at clearance prices?" They can spend some time discussing this, either in small groups or in the larger group.

- As they give answers, try to summarize their comments into short phrases. Use the marker to write the words on separate pieces of paper and set out on the empty table. You will probably collect a set of words such as "broken," "outdated," "returned," "ugly" and so on.

Step 2

- As you continue this activity, say something like this: "It's easy to sort out items based on value. While you might have a few questions, it's typically easy to note which items in a store have greater value and worth and which have less value and could easily be discounted. I have noticed, however, that sometimes in life we do the same thing. Not only do we sort out items as being valuable or not valuable, but we also tend to sort people that way! In fact, it's tempting at times to put people on the 'clearance table.' You might be tempted to sort people by size, ability, appearance, background, financial resources, or other factors."

■ At this point, make sure you tell a personal story about a time when you felt that someone had put *you* on the clearance table . . . how perhaps *you* were considered to be a "discounted" person.

Step 3

■ Give everyone a piece of paper and a pen or pencil. Ask them to write down a time when they felt like they had been sorted onto the clearance table. Make it clear that they don't need to share these with the group unless they choose to do so.

Step 4

■ Have the group imagine this next step with you. You're all back at the store after the clearance table has been set up. Then a very important person walks in. This person ignores all the other items in the store but absolutely adores the items on the clearance table. The person picks up each item and exclaims about it. He decides to put a special label on each item of merchandise.

■ At this point, pick up the papers with characteristics of clearance items written on them. For every negative phrase, cross it out and write something opposite instead. If it says "broken," write "priceless." If it says "returned," write "Mine forever," and so on.

■ Tell the group that when the store manager sees this, she tells you to put those items back on the shelves and charge full price—maybe even more! These are no longer discounted objects; they are very valuable.

Step 5

■ As a group, talk about how God does that for us. While we have differing strengths, weaknesses, talents, appearances, and backgrounds, we all have the same God, who picks up each one of his children and puts *his* labels on us. These labels say "handmade by God," "important," "honored," "member of the body of Christ," "salt

and light of the world," "indispensable," "dearly loved child," "forgiven," "mine."

■ As you mention each set of words, peel off the corresponding sticker from one of the preprinted sticker sheets and place it somewhere on your clothing. At the end, you will be covered with words that God uses to describe you—and everyone else in the group.

Step 6

■ (Individualize this part to fit the situation in your group). Say something similar to this, "It's easy to put people on the clearance table. People do it all the time. We all can remember a time when we felt that others had placed us in that category. I shared a story earlier about that. But look at me. I'm a 'dearly loved child, important, indispensable (continue reading the God labels stuck all over you).' It's clear that I don't belong on that clearance table—you can see who I really am. Does anyone else want to share the story you wrote down earlier of feeling like you were sorted onto that table?"

■ As the individual talks, cover them with the same set of God labels you are wearing. Then say, "You never should have been put on that clearance table. God has placed great value and worth on you! We can see who you really are. I know that this can frequently happen to persons with disabilities. People take one look and decide that the person in the wheelchair or the person who might have an intellectual disability must not be as valuable as others in the group."

■ Depending on the situation, you may be able to highlight a member of the group and ask that person to relate a story his or her parents may have told you—with permission, of course—about feeling like they had been sorted onto that clearance table. After that person has shared, make sure to place a full set of God labels on that individual. Say, "It's clear that you don't belong on that clearance table—we can see who you really are."

Step 7

- Say, "As we learn and have fun together this year, it's important for us to remember who we are and whose we are. These words that God speaks over us are like that very important person coming into the store, picking up the items, and admiring them. God has done that for each one of us. It's not logical to have a dearly loved child of God placed on a clearance table. We don't belong there! We also should never place anyone else there! We all have weaknesses; we all have areas of sin. We all have things that are hard for us to do. But in Christ, God gives us these words that describe who we are. And as we gather together this year, we will see clearly who we really are."

Step 8

- Pass out the remaining God labels to each person and ask them to help create a frame for a group picture. Have them peel off those words and stick them like a collage around the outside edges of a larger piece of paper that you have hung on the wall. The words will form a frame around the border.

- Invite each person to come up to write his or her name inside the frame with a colored marker (if you have a large group, several kids can do this at one time.) Or gather everyone together and take a group photo to place inside the frame later after you print it.

- As you monitor interactions throughout the group over time, feel free to refer back to this visual wall display.

Extension Ideas

The phrases describing who we are in Christ are written in Scripture. Spend some time locating the phrases and even adding additional ones to the frame.

It's possible that the activity will also lead to a time of discussion and prayer on granting or asking forgiveness. It's also possible that you will discover children who have put themselves on the clearance table. No one else has placed them there, but they see themselves as a "discounted" person. It's important to teach people not only to see others through the frame of God labels but to see ourselves through those labels as well.

Adaptations for Differing Abilities

You'll want to tailor this lesson plan to the abilities of the children in your group so that every child can participate in a meaningful way. Need help? See the Activity Substitution Guide on page 73.

Activity Substitution Guide

Each child in your group is a God-designed mixture of strengths and challenges. In any given activity, some children may flourish and others may flounder. If you have children in your group who find certain activities challenging, here are some ideas for substitutions.

Activities the child finds challenging	Substitutions you can make
Cutting	Use a spring-loaded scissors or small-sized scissors.
	Give the child a set of precut items.
	Give the child a set of pictures with only minimal cutting left to do on each item.
	Outline with thick marker the lines and curves that need to be cut.
	Have the child "hop on your hand" and do the cutting together.
Writing	Use a pencil or pen the child finds successful (larger, weighted, triangular, mechanical).
	Raise the writing surface to a 45-degree angle.
	Put a pencil grip on the pencil or pen.
	Give the child a writing buddy. Have both children write their names on the paper to signify ownership. Then ask one to do the writing after they agree on an answer together. Make a copy and send it home with both children.
	Assign a "secretary" to do the writing for the child.
	Downsize. Assign the child to write the answer to number 1 while the others write the answers to numbers 2-5.
Coloring	Use larger or smaller crayons according to what helps the child.
	Outline in marker the object(s) you want the child to color.
	Have the child "hop on your hand" as you color together.
	Precolor the page, but leave a few items blank.
	Assign a buddy to play "Simon Says," where the child tells the buddy what item to color and which color to use.
Speaking	Give a choice to write or speak the answer.
	Have a set of pictures or objects available and ask the child to point to the picture or item.
	Ask questions that can be answered with a head nod or shake or with a thumbs-up or thumbs-down response.
	Ask for a response that requires a movement for an answer.

Listening	Provide as many visuals as possible.
	Add signs and gestures to your presentation.
	Give directions one at a time.
	Ask the child to repeat the directions one at a time.
	Show a finished model for children to follow.
	Use an amplifying system to highlight the voice of the speaker.
Looking	Describe with words the items you are showing or holding up.
	Reproduce the visuals on high-contrast paper (black on yellow).
	Enlarge the visuals.
	Find items the individual can touch or hold.
Moving	If the person has difficulty using a certain body part, substitute another activity. Instead of running to the area, the person can point to the area. Or instead of pointing, they can look at the item.
	Assign a pair where the individual completes one portion while the buddy completes the challenging movement.
	Alter the activity for all in the group so that movement is eliminated or changed to something all can do together.
Reading	Read to the individual.
	Record what needs to be read and play the recording.
	Assign a buddy and have one person be the reader and one person be the listener and picture-watcher.
	Prepare and have the child practice the reading passage ahead of time.
	Color-code or highlight what should be read.

Be creative! Use this list as a jumping-off point to discover what works for each child in your group.

Patterns

making friends

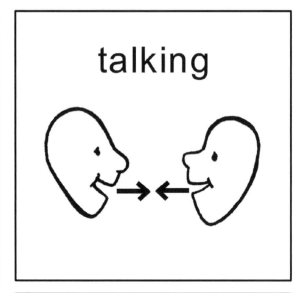

talking

knowing Jesus

remembering

problem solving

understanding time

moving

writing

paying attention

ears

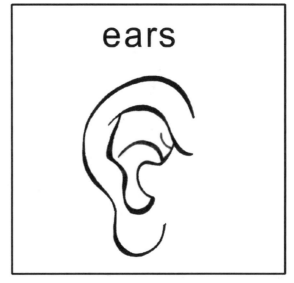

eyes

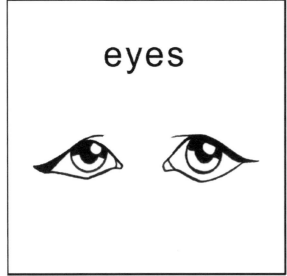

drawing

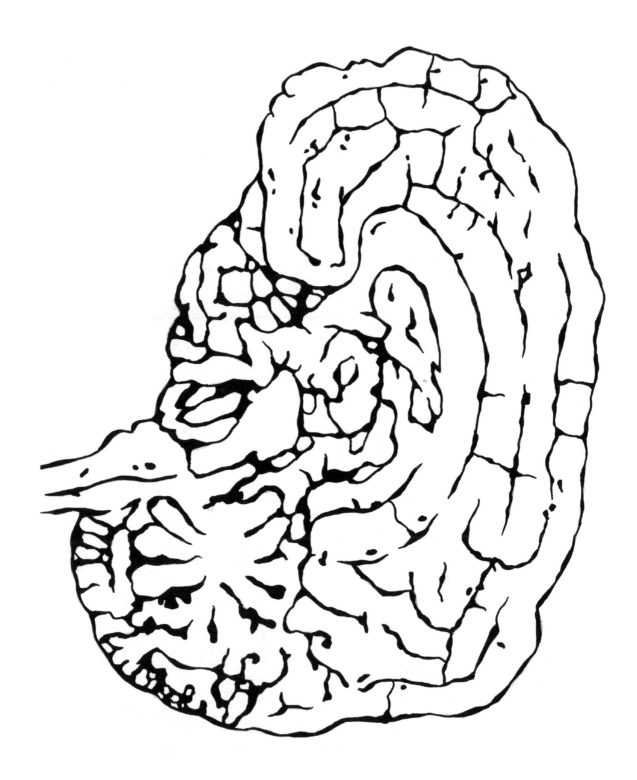

walking

crying

reading

sleeping

eating

crawling

Chapter 4 lesson plan: Hearing Impairment

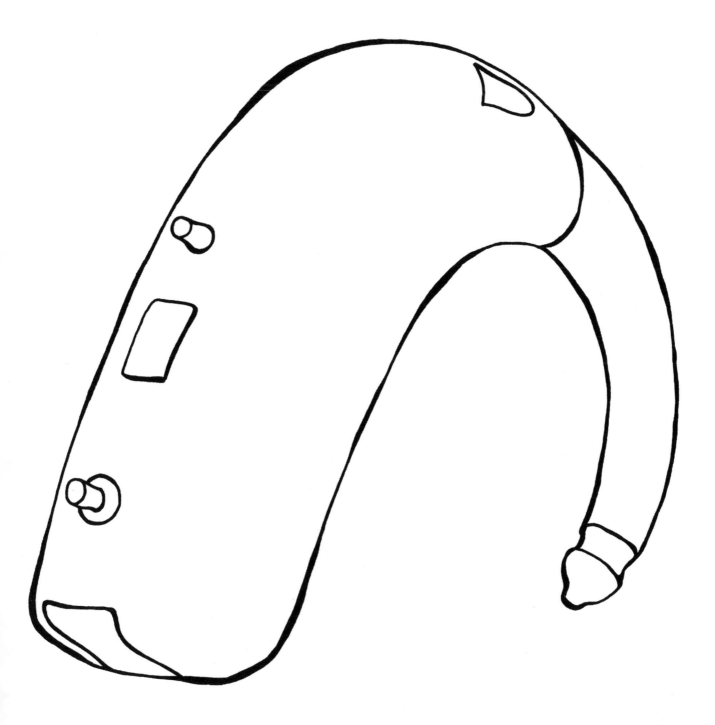

Chapter 4 lesson plan: Visual Impairment

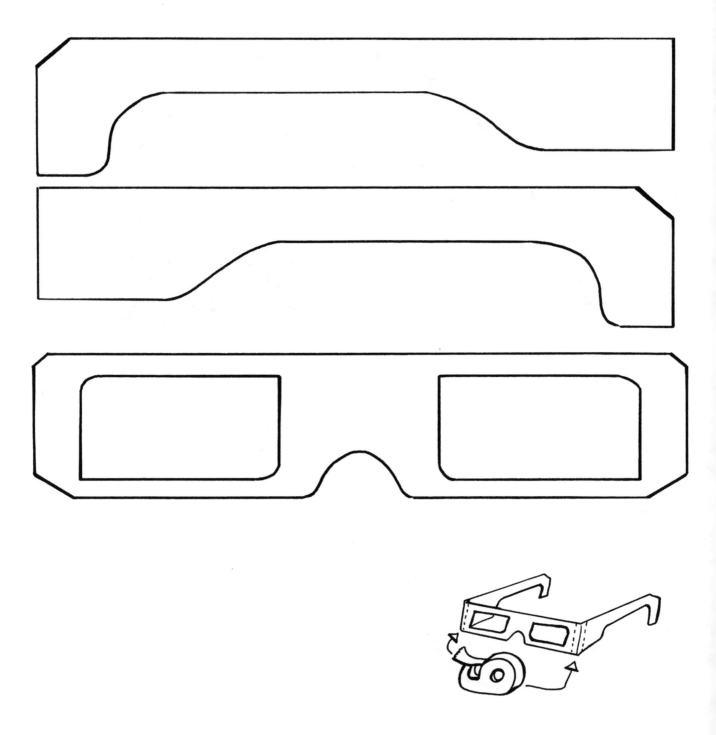

eyes

ears

fingers

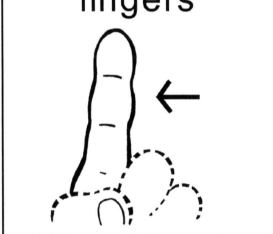

Resources

Anderson, Neil T. *The Bondage Breaker*. (Eugene: Harvest House Publishers, 2000.)

Attention Deficit/Hyperactivity Disorder. (Washington, D.C.: National Information Center for Children and Youth with Disabilities, 2012.)

Autism. (Washington, D.C.: National Information Center for Children and Youth with Disabilities, 2010.)

Blindness/Visual Impairment. (Washington, D.C.: National Information Center for Children and Youth with Disabilities, 2004.)

Carle, Eric. *The Very Hungry Caterpillar*. (New York: The Putnam & Grosset Group, 1969.)

Carter, Erik W. *Including People with Disabilities in Faith Communities*. (Baltimore: Paul H. Brookes Publishing Co., 2007.)

Deafness and Hearing Loss. (Washington, D.C.: National Information Center for Children and Youth with Disabilities, 2010.)

DeYoung, Terry A., and Mark Stephenson. *Inclusion Handbook: Everybody Belongs, Everybody Serves*. (Grand Rapids: Reformed Church Press, 2011.)

Down Syndrome. (Washington, D.C.: National Information Center for Children and Youth with Disabilities, 2010.)

Emotional Disturbance. (Washington, D.C.: National Information Center for Children and Youth with Disabilities, 2010.)

Fleming, Virginia. *Be Good to Eddie Lee*. (New York: The Putnam & Grosset Group, 1993.)

Intellectual Disabilities. (Washington, D.C.: National Information Center for Children and Youth with Disabilities, 2011.)

Kutscher, Martin L. M.D., *Kids in the Syndrome Mix of ADHD, LD, Asperger's, Tourette's, Bipolar, and More!* (Philadelphia: Jessica Kingsley Publishers, 2005.)

Learning Disabilities. (Washington, D.C.: National Information Center for Children and Youth with Disabilities, 2011.)

Levine, Mel. *Educational Care, 2nd Edition*. (Cambridge, Mass.: Educators Publishing Service, Inc., 2001.)

Luurtsema, Kimberley and Barbara J. Newman. *The G.L.U.E. Training Manual*. (Wyoming, MI: CLC Network, 2009.)

Newman, Barbara J. *Autism and Your Church*. (Grand Rapids, MI: Friendship Ministries, 2011.)

Newman, Barbara J. *Autism: A Christian Response Training DVD*. (Wyoming, MI: CLC Network: 2012.)

Newman, Barbara J. *Behavior Management Playing Field Training DVD*. (Wyoming, MI: CLC Network, 2012.)

Newman, Barbara J. *Body Building: Devotions to Celebrate Inclusive Community, 2nd Edition*. (Wyoming, MI: CLC Network, 2011.)

Newman, Barbara J. *Church Welcome Story*. (Wyoming, MI: CLC Network, 2009.)

Newman, Barbara J. *Circle of Friends Training Manual*. (Wyoming, MI: CLC Network 2010.)

Newman, Barbara J. *Disability Emphasis Week: Devotions for Families*. (Available online at crcna.org; search for "disability week family devotions.")

Newman, Barbara J. *Inclusion Toolkit Training DVD*. (Wyoming, MI: CLC Network, 2012.)

Newman, Barbara J. *Making Heaven a Noisier Place Training DVD*. (Wyoming, MI: CLC Network, 2012.)

Richardson, Susan. *Child by Child: Supporting Children with Learning Differences and Their Families*. (Harrisburg: Morehouse Publishing, 2011.)

Severe and/or Multiple Disabilities. (Washington, D.C.: National Information Center for Children and Youth with Disabilities, 2006.)

Speech and Language Impairments. (Washington, D.C.: National Information Center for Children and Youth with Disabilities, 2011.)

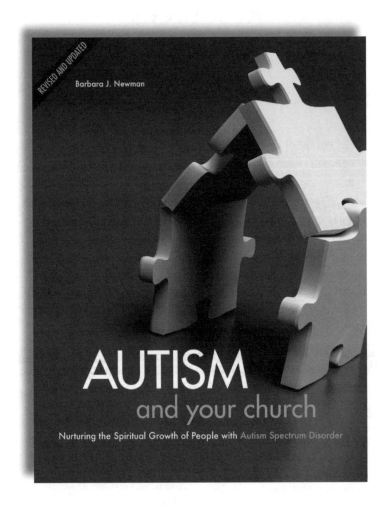

One of every five people lives with chronic illness or disability and the social isolation that often results. Unfortunately, churches often don't know how to meet their needs. This book helps church leaders and care team members understand the implications of living with a chronic condition and provides practical tips for developing a caring and compassionate ministry. Includes discussion questions and leader notes for a one-session workshop. A great resource to study with your congregational care team.

$6.99
FaithAliveResources.org